FIE

FIELD DAYS

An Anthology of Poetry

edited by Angela King and Susan Clifford for
Common Ground

With a Foreword by Adam Nicolson

Green Books

First published in 1998
by Green Books Ltd
Foxhole, Dartington
Totnes, Devon TQ9 6EB

in association with Common Ground
P.O. Box 25309, London NW5 1ZA

Cover design by Rick Lawrence
Cover illustration © Clifford Harper 1997

Text printed web offset by Biddles Ltd, Guildford, Surrey
on Five Seasons 100% recycled paper

British Library Cataloguing in Publication Data
Field Days: an anthology of poetry.

I. Poetry in English. Special subjects. Fields. Anthologies

I. King, Angela, II. Clifford, Susan

ISBN 1 870098 73 0

Contents

Preface by Angela King and Sue Clifford   *11*

Foreword by Adam Nicolson   *13*

The Poems, A-Z by title

Advice	W. H. Davies	*19*
An Epitaph at Great Torrington, Devon	Anonymous	*19*
April	Herbert Read	*19*
As I Watch'd the Ploughman Ploughing	Walt Whitman	*20*
Barrow	John Greening	*20*
The Barrow	Anthony Thwaite	*21*
Beggar's Luck	W. H. Davies	*22*
Black Furrow, Gray Furrow	George Mackay Brown	*22*
Bread and Butter Letter	Michael Hamburger	*23*
The Bright Field	R. S. Thomas	*24*
Brockhampton	Alison Brackenbury	*25*
Brown Earth Look	Ivor Gurney	*25*
Burning Off	Maureen Duffy	*26*
By Rail through the Earthly Paradise, Perhaps Bedfordshire	Denise Levertov	*28*
The Cabbage Field	Denise Levertov	*29*
Childhood Memory	Kathleen Raine	*30*
The Clover Fields	E. J. Scovell	*30*
'Consider the Lilies of the Field'	Christina Rossetti	*31*
Cornish Acre	A. L. Rowse	*32*
Cowslips and Larks	W. H. Davies	*33*
Cynddylan on a Tractor	R. S. Thomas	*33*

The Earthworm	Harry Edmund Martinson	34
English Wild Flowers	Elizabeth Jennings	34
A Farm Picture	Walt Whitman	35
Farmworker	P. J. Kavanagh	36
Fetching Cows	Norman MacCaig	36
A Field	E. J. Scovell	37
A Field in June	Gerald Bullett	38
The Field	Ruth Fainlight	38
The Field	Christopher Wiseman	39
Field and Forest	Randall Jarrell	40
Field Day	W. R. Rodgers	41
Field Names	Clive Sansom	42
The Field, Tomorrow	George MacBeth	43
Fieldwalking	Norman Jackson	44
Flints	Jeremy Hooker	45
Friendly are Meadows	Ivor Gurney	46
Gander Down	Jeremy Hooker	46
Glanmore Sonnets 1	Seamus Heaney	47
The Gleaners	Martyn Crucefix	48
Grasshoppers	John Clare	49
A Happy Life	W. H. Davies	49
Hares at Play	John Clare	50
Hares Boxing	Roger Garfitt	51
Harvest	Frances Cornford	52
Harvest	James Crowden	53
Harvest	Pamela Gillilan	54
Harvest at Mynachlog	Gillian Clarke	55
Harvest Hymn	John Betjeman	56
Hay	Gillian Clarke	57
Haymaking	Edward Thomas	58
Hertfordshire	John Betjeman	59
The Hill Field	Donald Davie	61

Home-Field	William Barnes	62
Home-thoughts, from Abroad	Robert Browning	63
Horses	Wendell Berry	63
Hunting Pheasants in a Cornfield	Robert Bly	66
I Got Two Vields	William Barnes	67
'I grant indeed that fields and flocks have charms' *from* The Village	George Crabbe	68
'In a summer season when the sun was mild' from The Vision of Piers Plowman	William Langland	68
In December	Ivor Gurney	69
'In early spring, when the ice on the snowy mountains' *from* The Georgics	Virgil	70
In Flanders Fields	John McCrae	72
In Summer	Denise Levertov	72
'In that open field' *from* 'East Coker'	T. S. Eliot	73
In the Fallow Field	Andrew Young	74
In the Fields	Charlotte Mew	75
The Invisible Globe	Jeremy Hooker	75
John Barleycorn	Traditional	76
The Land	Rudyard Kipling	78
The Licorice Fields at Pontefract	John Betjeman	80
Linum	Alison Brackenbury	81
Lost Acres	Robert Graves	82
The Mare	Vernon Watkins	83
Meadow in Drought	Ruth Bidgood	83
To Meddowes	Robert Herrick	84
Millom Cricket Field	Norman Nicholson	85
The Mores	John Clare	86
Mowing	Robert Frost	88
My Meadow	Hayden Carruth	88
Naming the Field	David Hart	90
Neutral	Jeremy Reed	92

The New Cemetery	Norman Nicholson	93
New Crops	Helen Dunmore	94
No Sprinkling of Bright Weeds	Geoffrey Grigson	95
Notes on a Field-Map	Kevin Crossley-Holland	96
O ubi campi!	Basil Bunting	97
The Old Showfield	Tom Rawling	98
On Merrow Down	John Burnside	100
On the Grasshopper and Cricket	John Keats	101
On the Hill	Andrew Young	102
Over the Fields	Maura Dooley	103
Pasturelands	Herbert Read	103
Pied Beauty	Gerard Manley Hopkins	104
Ploughing	Clive Sansom	104
Ploughing the Roughlands	Helen Dunmore	105
The Ploughman	Patrick Kavanagh	106
Ploughman, Ploughman	Andrew Young	106
Ploughman and Whales	George Mackay Brown	107
A Poet Visits	Frances Horovitz	108
The Poplar-Field	William Cowper	109
Question in a Field	Louise Bogan	109
Rhubarb Rhubarb	Ruth Pitter	110
Riley	Charles Causley	110
St Luke's Summer	Norman Nicholson	112
Scarecrow	Clive Sansom	112
The Scarecrow	Michael Hamburger	113
The Scarecrow	Andrew Young	114
Scything	James Crowden	114
September	John Burnside	115
Skylark	Katrina Porteous	116
The Sky Lark	John Clare	116
The Soldier	Rupert Brooke	117
Song	William Blake	118

Stacking the Straw	Amy Clampitt	118
Struggling Wheat	Ruth Pitter	120
Stubble Fires	Peter Scupham	121
The Sun used to Shine	Edward Thomas	122
They are Ploughing	E. J. Scovell	123
The Thing in the Gap-Stone Stile	Alice Oswald	123
Thistle	Laurie Lee	124
Three Kinds of Pleasures	Robert Bly	125
'Through all the meadows'	Sylvia Townsend-Warner	126
To a Fat Lady Seen from the Train	Frances Cornford	127
To a Mouse	Robert Burns	127
Turnip-Heads	Fleur Adcock	129
'Up on the downs'	John Masefield	129
Up There	Ivor Gurney	130
The Viking Field	Kevin Crossley-Holland	131
A Voice of Summer	Norman MacCaig	132
Waiting for the Harvester	Peter Abbs	133
Walking on Sunday	N. S. Jackson	134
Watercolour of Grantchester Meadows	Sylvia Plath	135
We Field-Women	Thomas Hardy	136
'We have walked so many times, my boy'	Wendell Berry	137
Woman in a Mustard Field	Alice Oswald	140

Acknowledgements	142
A-Z list of Poets and their Poems with Sources and Acknowledgements	144
About Common Ground	157
Common Ground's Manifesto for Fields	158
Publications by Common Ground	160

Preface

Perhaps we should have anticipated the richness we have found, for fields are one of our oldest inventions: they offer thousands of years of testimony to hard work and manifold pacts we are capable of making with nature. Having created the anthology *Trees Be Company* in 1989, we imagined that poetry about fields would be harder to find—this has not proved so.

Many of us associate fields with childhood memories of nature at its most generous and resplendent—the cultural fashioning of these enclosures, its gentle dynamism, helped nature, over centuries, to build richness and particularity with us.

The speed, scale and purposes of change over the last two generations has changed everything. The impatience for every inch to produce a crop of cash in the shortest time, with the fashions for chemical and intensive agriculture, have demonized domestic animals, homogenized landscape, ousted wild life and stripped farmers of their own history in the land. Hostile takeovers of 'green field sites' by development of all kinds fail to give value to the significance and meaning which fields have for us, in their crude equations of cost and benefit.

And yet, fields can exemplify the most sophisticated mutuality between nature and culture which we are capable of creating and sustaining. We need to extend that understanding, continuity and conscious care which the best of them represent. Shaming statistics—only 3% of hay meadows, pastoral jewels in the crown, have survived since 1975, and skylarks have plummeted by 58% in 25 years—should not have the last word.

Common Ground's work has tried to weave disparate strands into a broadloom of argument to refocus debate on the integrity of our relations with the land in our *Manifesto for Fields*.

And this collection of poetry is another kind of manifesto—it offers a glimpse into the deep relationships which we are capable of making between the cultural and natural world, and stands as further testimony from the many who do care, to the rest of us who must add action to words.

Angela King & Sue Clifford
Common Ground, July 1998

Foreword

I have eleven fields, all grass, all hedged, all part of one farm. They are all, to a stranger, pretty much of a piece, and pretty much the same as other fields on other farms around here, where cattle graze and buttercups grow and hedges are cut each sodden March and the hay made each burning July. They are part of what strangers call 'a landscape', that distant word which no one ever applies to a place they know or love but which drapes the singularity of convenience over every local reality. Landscape, prospect, scenery, view: synonyms for ignorance.

These words dissolve when you know a place. With knowledge the landscape becomes its constituent parts, breaks up into farms and farms into their woods, tracks and rough places, the stream beds where the moss is thick and nightingales sing, damp places where rushes grow and after rain the water collects in little grass-drowning pools.

That is the level at which I know my farm. There's no need for a satellite fix of what grows where, of the fertile or infertile patches, the over-enriched dock-thickened parts or those where the soil has disappeared to a sliver as thin as the quick under a fingernail, the grasses and daisies growing straight and thin out of the naked clay. I know all these things yard by yard. I know what every notched place here looks like at any time of year. I have in my mind a full house of seasons for every cranny. The Northumberland poet Katrina Porteous has written about the fishermen on her North Sea coast carrying in their minds the complete undersea geography of their chosen fishing grounds, an estate never seen but constantly imagined, the mind's eye crawling and feeling its way, as careful as a lobster, with the antennae as advance guards, through the fields of bladderwrack and the oceans of kelp. For me, with every other season except the present one, it is like that here: the future presence of a splash of garlic by the fallen oak down towards the sunny edge of the bluebell wood; the future presence of those bluebells collapsed and flowerless, as though a passing flood had flattened and drowned them; the future rattle of the acorns sprayed by autumn winds and beating without rhythm through the trunks of the hornbeam underwood; the future absence of any single thing to lift the spirit in the deep and rain-soaked blackness of those winter trees. The whole year co-exists in a known place. It is what distinguishes the known from the casually glanced at or the coolly wandered through.

Fields, though, are not quite like this. The field is a halfway house, halfway between the detail of those intimately known places and the ignorance of a landscape view. A field is an anthology of details. Every field does, after all, have a name which the microdots of a known place never do. My eleven are the Way field—which we now in fact call Rosie's field because my daughter Rosie had her first birthday party there in the summer after we arrived at this farm—Beech Meadow, Toyland, the Orchard, Cottage Field, Long Field, Jim's Field, Slip Field, Target Field, Hollow Flemings and Great Flemings. Those names adumbrate a whole sequence of lives lived here, including ours. I planted the orchard four winters ago. I don't know what it was called before. Target Field was given that name in the war when some Canadian soldiers, billeted here, set up a rifle range there. Its earlier name has gone. Jim's Field was rented by the gamekeeper of the local estate, Jim Mepham, to graze his bullocks in the Thirties and Forties. Beech Meadow does have one beech tree growing in one of its hedges but I have no idea why the field carries the name. Perhaps there was an earlier, bigger beech there once, of which this tree—a curious and magical thing, growing within a foot of and the same age as an oak so that the arms of each are intertwined with the other—is the less conspicuous descendant. Slip Field slipped a few decades ago when it was deep ploughed for the first time. Toyland is a misheard corruption of Tyeland, a Kent and Sussex dialect word meaning common land, which it must once have been but I have no idea when, perhaps before the farm was made in the 16th century. Long Field is not the longest but is probably one of the oldest. I guess its name preserves the memory of a time when fewer fields had been cut from the wood here and it was indeed the longest, a sinuous run along a stream that was chosen for the parish boundary. And the Flemings remain a mystery. Certainly there were Flemings near here in the 16th century, immigrants skilled in the making of glass and the forging of iron. Beyond that, I know nothing.

These layered changes, this dialogue with the place that the names record, this mixture of memory and oblivion, fragmentary preservation and partial erasure, comes near the heart of fields' significance for us. They are a form of current memorial, a marriage of life and permanence, halfway between now and then, between the made and the given, between the local and the abstract; beautiful, in Ivor Gurney's astonishing word, for their 'usualty'.

Recognising that beauty, or even searching for beauty in the form of the field, is a modern taste. Earlier visions of rural beauty did not on the whole involve the field. The Arcadian idea was either of a liberal and liberated woodland existence or, with the invention of the attitude encapsulated by the ha-ha, an open savannah at ease with itself, wood-pasture without the definition or restriction of the wall, gate or hedge. At the height of Romanticism, this appetite for freedom stretched to the untrammelled heights. "The farther I ascend from animated nature," Coleridge wrote early in 1803, looking back on his ecstatic fellside experiences of the previous summer, "from men, and cattle, & the common birds of the woods, & fields, the greater becomes in me the Intensity of the feeling of Life."

That primitivism and that relish for the envelopingly wild dominated the 19th century but became at least suspect after the First World War. I have a feeling, although this is perhaps difficult to substantiate, that the Western Front changed the meaning of wildness. The merciless wildness of a place, previously seen in the wake of Coleridge as an entrancing prospect, became in Flanders and on the Somme a maddening and horrific reality. The total absence of safety in what was called 'the devastated zone', and the complete remaking of the previously agricultural world in which that war was fought, may in themselves have stimulated the hunger for the field, for the steadiness, persistence and humanity of the field which this anthology celebrates. It should be remembered that when the Flemish inhabitants of Passchendaele returned there after the war, they could not find it. The village, farms and fields they had known were no longer there. They did not know where to rebuild. They chose a place as well as they could but it was a guess. When Flanders was again surveyed in the 1920s, it was found that Passchendaele, with its church, town hall, shops, square, houses, streets, its network of roads and outlying farms, the willow-lined ditches and the potato and maize fields between them, had moved on average, by about 300 metres, a new geography in a changed world.

"Poetry," Auden wrote, "is a momentary stay against confusion," and in that, I think, at least for the modern mind, a field and a poem are the same. They are both, of their essence, cut off from and even set against what surrounds them. Each is a small world defined by its boundaries. In each is a particular vision, a particular history, a difference from "the waste sad time stretching before and after." But each holds something else within its boundaries. The essence of a field is that the cultural accommodates the natural there: the field is a poem to symbiosis and a human contract with the natural. A poem makes that accommodation too. The searing Gloucester-surrealist language of a Gurney poem, surely the hero of this anthology, is the equivalent of those places in a field where a hatch of common blues is flittering over the vetches, or a bunch of rushes at night takes on the outlines of a deer, head bowed to graze. In both, the other is held within a containing form. That is the reason, in the end, that we think of fields now, after Passchendaele, after Buchenwald, as such good places. We are neither alien nor omnipotent there. They belong to us but there are things beyond us in them. We shape them, make them, control them, name them but they are not what we are. They are our partners. Or at least that is the ideal condition. Industrialised farming is so often painful and disturbing precisely because it involves the breaking of that contract and the chemical reduction of partner to slave. As often seen in this anthology, there can be a better way than that, a concordance between the human and the natural, a mutuality, which as Wendell Berry has written, is the essence of music, goodness and hope:

> Now every move
> answers what is still.
> This work of love rhymes
> living and dead. A dance
> is what this plodding is.
> A song, whatever is said.

Adam Nicolson

I found the poems in the fields
and only wrote them down

John Clare

Advice

Now, you two eyes, that have all night been sleeping,
Come into the meadows, where the lambs are leaping;
See how they start at every swallow's shadow
That darts across their faces and their meadow.
See how the blades spring upright, when the Sun
Takes off the weight of raindrops, one by one.
See how a shower, that freshened leaves of grass,
Can make that bird's voice fresher than it was.
See how the squirrels lash the quiet trees
Into a tempest, where there is no breeze!
Now, you two eyes, that have all night been sleeping,
Come into the meadows, where the lambs are leaping.

W. H. Davies

An Epitaph at Great Torrington, Devon

Here lies a man who was killed by lightning;
He died when his prospects seemed to be brightening.
He might have cut a flash in this world of trouble,
But the flash cut him, and he lies in the stubble.

Anonymous

April

To the fresh wet fields
and the white
froth of flowers

Came the wild errant
swallows with a scream.

Herbert Read

As I Watch'd the Ploughman Ploughing

As I watch'd the ploughman ploughing,
Or the sower sowing in the fields, or the harvester
    harvesting,
I saw there too, O life and death, your analogies;
(Life, life is the tillage, and Death is the harvest according.)

Walt Whitman

Barrow

Our brittle bones were chilled to envy
even of the bones in Stoney Littleton
Long Barrow, where I had tapped

at a tubercular farmhouse to beg
and stood awaiting something at the entrance
to a chamber, sealed and on the list

for surgery. But there was no key.
And since our torch was not charged up, we
gazed down a narrow beam of darkness

imagining ourselves through there, to turn
and find this glow, as—looking back—
one might spot brilliance in a dark age.

Across the valley, the sun quite lost
in a serge-grey labyrinth, a whole field
once filled with hay is landfill now:

yellow skips, black plastic, keening
white gulls, and us—powerless
above our age's burial mound.

John Greening

The Barrow

In this high field strewn with stones
I walk by a green mound,
Its edges sheared by the plough.
Crumbs of animal bone
Lie smashed and scattered round
Under the clover leaves
And slivers of flint seem to grow
Like white leaves among green.
In the wind, the chestnut heaves
Where a man's grave has been.

Whatever the barrow held
Once, has been taken away:
A hollow of nettles and dock
Lies at the centre, filled
With rain from a sky so grey
It reflects nothing at all.
I poke in the crumbled rock
For something they left behind
But after that funeral
There is nothing at all to find.

On the map in front of me
The gothic letters pick out
Dozens of tombs like this,
Breached, plundered, left empty,
No fragments littered about
Of a dead and buried race
In the margins of histories.
No fragments: these splintered bones
Construct no human face,
These stones are simply stones.

In museums their urns lie
Behind glass, and their shaped flints
Are labelled like butterflies.
All that they did was die,

And all that has happened since
Means nothing to this place.
Above long clouds, the skies
Turn to a brilliant red
And show in the water's face
One living, and not these dead.

Anthony Thwaite

Beggar's Luck

Where did you sleep in the Country, Lad?
  'It was a field of hay.'
Did you sleep soundly there, and well?
  'Till after break of day.'

Where did you sleep in the City, Lad—
  Where did you rest your bones?
'They gave me neither straw nor feather,
  And drove me away with stones.'

W. H. Davies

Black Furrow, Gray Furrow

From the black furrow, a fecund
Whisper of dust,
From the gray furrow, a sudden
Gleam and thrust,
Crossings of net and ploughshare,
Fishbone and crust.

George Mackay Brown

Bread and Butter Letter

to Philip and Barbara Rawson

Bread is the fields of wheat
Where partridges creaked in flight,
Faint hum of daytime tractor,
The fidgeted drum of night;
Butter the mushroomed pastures,
Meadow and muddy patch,
Parched where the clumps and the mounds are,
Sodden in hollow and ditch.

And water: the shallow river
With willow, lily and rush,
Then the sudden pool, no wider,
Though deep as diver could wish.

These are not you—nor yours
To keep or to give away:
This barn you did not build
Nor saved the roof from decay;
Yet its ruin's pattern grew fertile
When the skeleton pierced your gaze
To be more than thatched in thought—
To leap alive from your eyes.

As from ridge and furrow we gather
The spirit behind the face
And lovers even must look for
Their love's true dwelling-place,
Praising the site of your tenure
I praise both mind and thing:
Their marriage, from which all beauty
And all creation spring.

May garden, orchard and meadow,
Cornfield, river and pool
Nourish your art and prove
As ever bountiful,

Lest the abstract cities wither
That primal intergrowth
Of outward form and inward,
Levelling all into death.

May all your bread be fields of wheat
And the dual pastures requite
With dual blessings your labour,
No daemon darken your site.

Michael Hamburger

The Bright Field

I have seen the sun break through
to illuminate a small field
for a while, and gone my way
and forgotten it. But that was the pearl
of great price, the one field that had
the treasure in it. I realize now
that I must give all that I have
to possess it. Life is not hurrying

on to a receding future, nor hankering after
an imagined past. It is the turning
aside like Moses to the miracle
of the lit bush, to a brightness
that seemed as transitory as your youth
once, but is the eternity that awaits you.

R. S. Thomas

Brockhampton

The land was too wet for ploughing; yet it is done.
Even the stones of the ridges lie sulky and brown.
The roads are a slide of mud. The wet sky
Is blank as the chink of the hawk's perfect eye.
A blink before the dark comes down
Drops the peregrine sun.

The land glows like an awkward face.
Broken posts, by which sheep graze
Shine pale as growing wood.
Above, the last crow's wings
Cannot frighten from my blood
The stubborn light of things.

Alison Brackenbury

Brown Earth Look

The youth burning couch grass is as tired
As muscle has right to bear and keeps work on
The brown earth slopes from the potato field to the wired
Sheep enclosure; and hidden high and white the sun.

Brown the sense of things, the light smoke blows across
The field face, light blue wisps of sweet bitter reek
Dear to the Roman perhaps, so old seems the dross
Burning of root, grass, wheat, so near, easy to seek.

Old is the land, a thousand generations
Have tilled there, sought with bright sweat the stuff of its
        bread.
Here one comes for the sense of fine books, revelations
Of beauty in usualty, found as well of heart as of head.

And all the tales of far Europe that come on one,
The sense of myriads tending the needings of life,
Are more to one than the near memory of battle gun.
Peace with its sorrow blots out the agonies of strife.

Ivor Gurney

Burning Off

Already autumn stains
a branch here and there
singles out leaves to stopper
their narrow veins with drought
though August's barely out.

Yesterday the yellow combine
tanked through corn
a minotaur carving
its own labyrinth
an iron whopstraw.

A cropped bright stubble
five o'clocks the fields
with stiff gold shafts
one night, then flares
is barbequed black.

Small pointed skulls cremate
slim runners' bones
stripped of sinew crumble
where the smoke stopped them
in their secret track.

These yearly harrowings
libations some god demands
are old as husbandry.
Once it was the delicate seed
of lovers in field or wood.

Now the ground trembles
under a metal stamp muting
the birds' alarm in the broken air.
At night the field is smeared black
under a drained moon.

Morning breaks
in a cold sweat of mist.
The motorway's a distant surf
I launch into. Returning
I drive through a still smutted sunset.

The junctions fall away
at summer's end.
That's where I turned off
in Spring when last year's seed
lay flecked with bonemeal in the ground.

Home again I walk
the unburnt stubble behind my house.
Tomorrow you fly back.
I should pour my heart's blood
out for luck. I do.

Maureen Duffy

By Rail through the Earthly Paradise, Perhaps Bedfordshire

The fishermen among the fireweed.

Towpath and humpbacked bridge. Cows
in one field, slabs of hay
ranged in another.

Common day
precious to me.
There's nothing else
to grasp.

The train
moves me past it too fast, not much,
just a little, I don't want
to stay for ever.
                    Horses,
three of them, flowing across a paddock
as wind flows over barley.

Oaks in parkland, distinct,
growing their shadows.
A man from Cairo across from me
reading *A Synopsis of Eye Physiology*.
The brickworks,
fantastical slender chimneys.

I'm not hungry,
not lonely. It seems
at times I want nothing,
no human giving and taking.
Nothing I see
fails to give pleasure,

no thirst for righteousness
dries my throat, I am silent
and happy, and troubled only
by my own happiness. Looking,

looking and naming. I wish the train now
would halt for me at a station in the fields,
(the name goes by
unread).
      In the deep aftermath
of its faded rhythm, I could become

a carved stone
set in the gates of the earthly paradise,

an angler's fly
lost in the sedge to watch the centuries.

Denise Levertov

The Cabbage Field

Both Taine and the inland English child
were mocked for their independent
comparison of the sea to a field of cabbages:

but does this field
of blue and green and purple curling
turmoil of ordered curves, reaching

out to the smoky twilight's immense
ambiguousness we call
horizon, resemble

anything but the sea?

Denise Levertov

Childhood Memory

Sunshine in morning field,
Sunshining king-cups,
My flowers, my sun—
'But you cannot look at the sun,
'No-one can look into the sun.'
And I said, 'I can,
'I can, it is golden, it is mine,'
And looked into a dancing ball of blood,
A pulsing darkness blind with blood.

Sunshine in morning field,
Sunshining king-cups,
My sun, my flowers—
'But you cannot gather those flowers,
'The calyx in your hand is speed, is power,
'Is multitude; in grain of golden dust
'Smaller than point of needle, there they dance,
'Unnumbered constellations as the stars
'They spin, they whirl, their infinitesimal space
'Empty as night where suns burn out in space.'

Dear and familiar face
That beamed on childhood,
Shining on morning field and flower smile
What emptiness veiled,
Chasms of inhuman darkness veiled.

Kathleen Raine

The Clover Fields

The fields are overcast with light at evening,
With marguerites increased, a chalk-white settling,
With mist of the damp breath of clover leaves and grasses
And slanting light reflected from their press of faces.

And close the earth shows parchment through, though netted
  over
With the fresh-dark entangled green and shade of clover,
The leaves ornate, the perfect narrow trefoils set
Thick as in tapestry, and little flowering yet.

And time stands like a soul; the summer's hardly flowing
Twilight stands in the fields that look towards their mowing,
Still as a man might stand in his own fields contemplating.
The meadows give their answer to this hour of waiting.

E. J. Scovell

'Consider the Lilies of the Field'

Flowers preach to us if we will hear:—
The rose saith in the dewy morn:
I am most fair;
Yet all my loveliness is born
Upon a thorn.
The poppy saith amid the corn:
Let but my scarlet head appear
And I am held in scorn;
Yet juice of subtle virtue lies
Within my cup of curious dyes.
The lilies say: Behold how we
Preach without words of purity.
The violets whisper from the shade
Which their own leaves have made:
Men scent our fragrance on the air,
Yet take no heed
Of humble lessons we would read.

But not alone the fairest flowers:
The merest grass
Along the roadside where we pass,
Lichen and moss and sturdy weed,
Tell of His love who sends the dew,
The rain and sunshine too,
To nourish one small seed.

Christina Rossetti

Cornish Acre

This is the field that looks to the south:
No words come to my mouth
To signify my dread
Of this field of the dead.

This is that field where on a time
Hope died in me,
Even as I looked out upon
The gay and smiling sea.

The blue and bitter southern sea
Laughed back at me and said
'Have you any recruits for me
From the field of the dead?'

Over the dark and echoing woods
I heard the bell toll nine,
And then I knew full well
The augury was mine.

O moving finger of time that writes
My name in water, on the sea,
Pause yet awhile upon this slope
Remembering me.

A. L. Rowse

Cowslips and Larks

I hear it said yon land is poor,
In spite of those rich cowslips there—
And all the singing larks it shoots
To heaven from the cowslips' roots.
But I, with eyes that beauty find,
And music ever in my mind,
Feed my thoughts well upon that grass
Which starves the horse, the ox, and ass.
So here I stand, two miles to come
To Shapwick and my ten-days-home,
Taking my summer's joy, although
The distant clouds are dark and low,
And comes a storm that, fierce and strong,
Has brought the Mendip Hills along:
Those hills that, when the light is there,
Are many a sunny mile from here.

W. H. Davies

Cynddylan on a Tractor

Ah, you should see Cynddylan on a tractor.
Gone the old look that yoked him to the soil;
He's a new man now, part of the machine,
His nerves of metal and his blood oil.
The clutch curses, but the gears obey
His least bidding, and lo, he's away
Out of the farmyard, scattering hens.
Riding to work now as a great man should,
He is the knight at arms breaking the fields'
Mirror of silence, emptying the wood
Of foxes and squirrels and bright jays.
The sun comes over the tall trees

33

Kindling all the hedges, but not for him
Who runs his engine on a different fuel.
And all the birds are singing, bills wide in vain,
As Cynddylan passes proudly up the lane.

R. S. Thomas

The Earthworm

Who really respects the earthworm,
the farmworker far under the grass in the soil.
He keeps the earth always changing.
He works entirely full of soil,
speechless with soil, and blind.

He is the underneath farmer, the underground one,
where the fields are getting on their harvest clothes.
Who really respects him,
this deep and calm earth-worker,
this deathless, gray, tiny farmer in the planet's soil.

Harry Edmund Martinson
(translated from the Swedish by Robert Bly)

English Wild Flowers

Forget the Latin names; the English ones
Are gracious and specific. Hedge-rows are
Quickening fast with vetch and cow-parsley.
And fast along the lawn the daisies rise
For chains or for the murdering lawn-mower.

Look everywhere, there is all botany
Laid between rising corn,
Infesting hay-fields. Look, the buttercup
Stares at the sun and seems to take a share
Of wealthy light. It glows beneath our chins.

Slim shepherd's purse is lost in dandelions,
Scabious will show a little later. See,
The dog-rose in the hedge. It dies at once
When you pluck it. Forget-me-nots disclose
Points of pure blue, the sovereign blue of sky.
And then there are the herbs.

Counting this floral beauty I grow warm
With patriotism. These are my own flowers,
Springing to pleasant life in my own nation.
The times are dark but never too dark for
An Eden Summer, this flower-rich creation.

Elizabeth Jennings

A Farm Picture

Through the ample open door of the peaceful country barn,
A sunlit pasture field with cattle and horses feeding,
And haze and vista, and the far horizon fading away.

Walt Whitman

Farmworker

Manhandled haybales not so yellow
As her hair, careful to leave a
Way for the nested swallow.
No stranger knocking the door
Of her stone nest received an answer:
Back to the window she stayed in her chair.

At walking-pace she rode her tractor
Like an old horse, you could follow
On foot her slumped back, her world
Of foxed perspex, watch the field
Barely grown in her windscreen,
Hedges come to attention, thorn by thorn.

For her to fail is like the season
Failing. Like a swallow, with less hesitation,
With no pause on a wire, she is gone.
Hedges lie doggo,
Hoping to die where they are,
To suffer birds and not have to answer.

P. J. Kavanagh

Fetching Cows

The black one, last as usual, swings her head
And coils a black tongue round a grass-tuft. I
Watch her soft weight come down, her split feet spread.

In front, the others swing and slouch; they roll
Their great Greek eyes and breathe out milky gusts
From muzzles black and shiny as wet coal.

The collie trots, bored, at my heels, then plops
Into the ditch. The sea makes a tired sound
That's always stopping though it never stops.

A haycart squats prickeared against the sky.
Hay breath and milk breath. Far out in the West
The wrecked sun founders though its colours fly.

The collie's bored. There's nothing to control . . .
The black cow is two native carriers
Bringing its belly home, slung from a pole.

Norman MacCaig

A Field

The field is bounded by four hedges built of may
Like stone. There, seen or unseen, the blossom is given,
Jets out from the deep springs of time all day;
Gone, is replenished. The scent floods for its season.

The grass in the square field is thin as wire, as dew;
Erect each grass, tarnished like colour under the moon,
With roseate mist, a fire-reflecting smoke, run through.

The short and brittle-seeming, cloudy grass
Peoples this framed and empty field as souls do heaven,
That travellers stare from the gate and cannot pass.

E. J. Scovell

A Field in June

Greed is dumb at sight of so much gold
As these immaculate cups lightly hold,
Nor do we finger with fever'd covetous look
The smooth meandering silver of the brook.
Untaxable bounties entering the mind's eye
From deep meadow and diamond-dropping sky,
Wool-gathering clouds and contemplating trees
Casting palpable shade, those and these
Spell silence, till a skylark, newly risen,
Lets joy and desire out of the dark prison.

Gerald Bullett

The Field

The field is trampled over utterly.
No hidden corner remains unchurned.
Unusable henceforth for pasture:
Sheep and cattle must feed elsewhere.

The field was torn by battle, dull
Explosions, trenches dug for shelter,
Vehicles which wheeled, reversed,
Hunted down the last resistance.

The field is strewn with bones and metal.
Earth which had not felt the air
During millennia, is now revealed
To every element and influence.

The undersoil surprises by its richness.
In battle's lull, at night, the farmer crawls
To estimate what might be salvaged
Of his lone field's potentiality.

If he survives, the field holds promise
Of great abundance, a yield astonishing,
Unprecedented as all he hopes for.
The field is fertile. He must survive.

Ruth Fainlight

The Field

That's where I saw the Lysander crash,
I tell my son,
when I was about your age.
There were two men in it,
both killed.

But it's flat, he says,
just a flat field.
Where's the hole?

I drive on,
hunched tightly around
that scarred place inside me,
cratered, still smoking,
that I can never show him.

Christopher Wiseman

Field and Forest

When you look down from the airplane you see lines,
Roads, ruts, braided into a net or web—
Where people go, what people do: the ways of life.

Heaven says to the farmer: 'What's your field?'
And he answers: 'Farming,' with a field,
Or: 'Dairy-farming,' with a herd of cows.
They seem a boy's toy cows, seen from this high.

Seen from this high,
The fields have a terrible monotony.

But between the lighter patches there are dark ones.
A farmer is separated from a farmer
By what farmers have in common: forests,
Those dark things—what the fields were to begin with.
At night a fox comes out of the forest, eats his chickens.
At night the deer come out of the forest, eat his crops.

If he could he'd make farm out of all the forest,
But it isn't worth it: some of it's marsh, some rocks,
There are things there you couldn't get rid of
With a bulldozer, even—not with dynamite.
Besides, he likes it. He had a cave there, as a boy;
He hunts there now. It's a waste of land,
But it would be a waste of time, a waste of money,
To make it into anything but what it is.

At night, from the airplane, all you see is lights,
A few lights, the lights of houses, headlights,
And darkness. Somewhere below, beside a light,
The farmer, naked, takes out his false teeth:
He doesn't eat now. Takes off his spectacles:
He doesn't see now. Shuts his eyes.
If he were able to he'd shut his ears,
And as it is, he doesn't hear with them.
Plainly, he's taken out his tongue: he doesn't talk.

His arms and legs: at least, he doesn't move them.
They are knotted together, curled up, like a child's.
And after he has taken off the thoughts
It has taken him his life to learn,
He takes off, last of all, the world.

When you take off everything what's left? A wish,
A blind wish; and yet the wish isn't blind,
What the wish wants to see, it sees.

There in the middle of the forest is the cave
And there, curled up inside it, is the fox.

He stands looking at it.
Around him the fields are sleeping: the fields dream.
At night there are no more farmers, no more farms.
At night the fields dream, the fields *are* the forest.
The boy stands looking at the fox
As if, if he looked long enough—
                    he looks at it.
Or is it the fox that's looking at the boy?
The trees can't tell the two of them apart.

Randall Jarrell

Field Day

The old farmer, nearing death, asked
To be carried outside and set down
Where he could see a certain field
'And then I will cry my heart out,' he said.

It troubles me, thinking about that man;
What shape was the field of his crying
In Donegal?

I remember a small field in Down, a field
Within fields, shaped like a triangle.
I could have stood there and looked at it
All day long.

And I remember crossing the frontier between
France and Spain at a forbidden point, and seeing
A small triangular field in Spain,
And stopping

Or walking in Ireland down any rutted by-road
To where it hit the highway, there was always
At this turning-point and abutment
A still centre, a V-shape of grass
Untouched by cornering traffic,
Where country lads larked at night.

I think I know what the shape of the field was
That made the old man weep.

W. R. Rodgers

Field Names

Our name-givers loved the World and loved the Word:
These two delights are only an ell apart.
Coupling, they gave birth to those field names
That map the earth in the language of the heart:

   'Wooden Cabbage', 'Three Men's Field',
   'Charity Bottom', 'Doom',
   'Perrymans', 'God's Blessing Green',
   'Fishponds' and 'Bramble Coomb'.
   'Reddleman's', 'Bedlam', 'Dancing Hill',
   'Troy Town', and 'Starvecrow Land',

'Lottery', 'Drummer's Castle', 'Fleet',
'Crocker's Knap', 'Flower-in-Hand'. . . .

Lavish as wildflowers in a Dorset hedgerow,
Fragrant as *their* names before the botanists came,
They startle the lawyers' deeds with their heart-language
And stake, in some fragment of England, their loving claim.

Clive Sansom

The Field, Tomorrow

I wanted the bare field out there to be mine.
Each day, at my typing, I saw the smooth line

Of the sycamores, breaking the sweep of the grass
To the farm and the river. I saw the sails pass

Far away, white and simple, where yachts moved at Thurne.
And I looked down, in pride, at my nearest stone urn.

From that urn to the sycamores, this was my land,
With the wide breadth of Norfolk stretched gold on each hand.

I had space, in my dream, and six acres to keep.
I had grass for my garden, and twenty new sheep.

It's all over. The field has been sold, to my friends,
And the dream of broad acres, all hope of it, ends.

At the auction I bid high, too high for my good,
And I'm glad that I missed it, at that price. I should

Have been forced into borrowing, bound to the shape
Of solicitor's ropes. But it still feels like rape

To see horses, brown horses, that other men own
(In my mind they seem galloping, sculptured like stone)

Out there in my bare field. I touch them, and weep,
And remember my dream, and the slow-moving sheep,

Their cold, lovely fleece, and their beautiful eyes,
And their mouths, low and cropping, surrounded by flies.

George MacBeth

Fieldwalking

The field quartered
By a nudge of ice,
Bends a place of spring water.
Half its hands still in the sea
Too many years passed
For this to be a known site.
Maps, grids, marker stones
Said this place is checked.
The path we took
Was familiar enough;
Oil had been abandoned there,
The heavy road feathered out
To wood and pond.
The Manor,
Sunk in a trough of wine.
Our field was clear enough,
The ridge and furrow
Pushed up under the plough,
A time so plain
To make our hands
Intrude.

Feeling the glass and stone
We take to plunder
Like a child to play.
And someone dark
Finds this, a place to stray.

Norman Jackson

Flints

They are ploughed out,
Or surface under surface

Washes away leaving the bleached
Floor of a sunken battleground.

Some are blue with the texture of resin,
The trap of a primeval shadow.

Others are green,
A relic of their origins.

The white one is
An eye closed on the fossil.

Worked in radial grooves
From the bulb of percussion

They shed brittle flakes.
The core with its brutal edge

Shaped the hand.

Jeremy Hooker

Friendly are Meadows

Friendly are meadows when the sun's gone in
And no bright colour spoils the broad green of grey,
And one's eyes rest looking to far Cotswold away
Under cloud ceilings whorled and most largely fashioned
With seventeenth-century curves of the tombstone way.
A day of softnesses, of comfort of no din, not passioned.
Sorrel makes rusty rest for the eyes, and the worn path,
Brave elms, and stiles, willows by dyked deep water-run—
North French general look, and a sort of bath
Of freshness—a light wrap of comfortableness
Over one's being, a sense as of music begun;
A slow gradual symphony of worthiness, fulfilledness.
But this is Cotswold, Severn: when these go stale
Then the all-universal and wide decree shall fail
Of world's binding, and earth's dust apart be loosed,
And man's worship of all grey comforts be abused,
To mere wonder at lightning and torrentous strong flying hail.

Ivor Gurney

Gander Down

The ploughed chalk sweeping
and shelving is a shore
from which the tide has just gone out.

Fine, black blades
of trees stand against depths
which the sun fills,
white and cold.

A big hare sits with ears up
on the rim of the world.

Larks rise singing from the ocean bed.

Jeremy Hooker

Glanmore Sonnets

For Ann Saddlemyer
our heartiest welcomer

I

Vowels ploughed into other: opened ground.
The mildest February for twenty years
Is mist bands over furrows, a deep no sound
Vulnerable to distant gargling tractors.
Our road is steaming, the turned-up acres breathe.
Now the good life could be to cross a field
And art a paradigm of earth new from the lathe
Of ploughs. My lea is deeply tilled.
Old ploughsocks gorge the subsoil of each sense
And I am quickened with a redolence
Of farmland as a dark unblown rose.
Wait then . . . Breasting the mist, in sowers' aprons,
My ghosts come striding into their spring stations.
The dream grain whirls like freakish Easter snows.

Seamus Heaney

The Gleaners

In the distance, a man
on a still horse gestures to where
the majority work, bending
like cattle to crop the ground.
Women scour the harvested field
for leavings, gathering bunches
of straw like bouquets, laying them
like wreathes into the sheaf, binding
the stooks for men to heave them
into a cart or on to the stacks
growing imperceptibly into the brown sky.

Nearer, in this stubble, two women
lean as one into the earth,
each pair of eyes knowing only the next
burnished filament, each
committed to the field, headscarves,
red and blue, caught
low in their bob-bobbing.

A third, winched almost upright,
pats her bouquet. The angle she makes
to the others, the one machine
of the gleaners, has her resolved
not to ask entry, nor acceptance,
but soon to insist they lift their heads,
scarved in the red and blue,
and imagine the artist.

Martyn Crucefix

Grasshoppers

Grasshoppers go in many a thrumming spring
And now to stalks of tasselled sour-grass cling,
That shakes and swees awhile, but still keeps straight;
While arching oxeye doubles with his weight.
Next on the cat-tail grass with farther bound
He springs, that bends until they touch the ground.

John Clare

A Happy Life

O what a life is this I lead,
Far from the hum of human greed;
Where Crows, like merchants dressed in black,
Go leisurely to work and back;
Where Swallows leap and dive and float,
And Cuckoo sounds his cheerful note;
Where Skylarks now in clouds do rave,
Half mad with fret that their souls have
By hundreds far more joyous notes
Than they can manage with their throats.
The ploughman's heavy horses run
The field as if in fright—for fun,
Or stand and laugh in voices shrill;
Or roll upon their backs until
The sky's kicked small enough—they think;
Then to a pool they go and drink.
The kine are chewing their old cud,
Dreaming, and never think to add
Fresh matter that will taste—as they
Lie motionless, and dream away.

I hear the sheep a-coughing near;
Like little children, when they hear
Their elders' sympathy—so these
Sheep force their coughs on me, and please;
And many a pretty lamb I see,
Who stops his play on seeing me,
And runs and tells his mother then.
Lord, who would live in towns with men,
And hear the hum of human greed—
With such a life as this to lead?

W. H. Davies

Hares at Play

The birds are gone to bed the cows are still
And sheep lie panting on each old mole hill
And underneath the willows grey green bough
Like toil a resting—lies the fallow plough
The timid hares throw daylights fears away
On the lanes road to dust and dance and play
Then dabble in the grain by nought deterred
To lick the dewfall from the barleys beard
Then out they sturt again and round the hill
Like happy thoughts dance squat and loiter still
Till milking maidens in the early morn
Gingle their yokes and start them in the corn
Through well known beaten paths each nimbling hare
Sturts quick as fear—and seeks its hidden lair

John Clare

Hares Boxing

for Nigel Wells

This way and that
goes the runaway furrow.
Nose to tail
goes the tunnel
in the grass.

Now the leader
swivels, jerks up his heels.
The trick flickers
along the rope of hares:
heels over head they go, head over heels.

It's the Saturday
after Valentine:
in Florey's Stores
the kids go
into huddles,

Oh! What did he put?
Go on, tell us! we *promise*
we won't tell.

Did she send you one?
    Did she?

Over the winter nothing has changed
but the land. The hedgerows
are in heaps for burning.
The owl's tree stands vacant
between the scars of smooth earth.

The sunlight falls on cleared spaces,
on the old lines. The hares meet
as they met before Enclosure, far out
in the drift of grasses, their fisticuffs
like tricks of the eye.

What catches the light, what the eye believes
is the rufous shoulder, the chest's white blaze:
what it sees are up on their haunches
the blaze throw its guard up, the shoulder
slide in a punch; two pugs that duel

stripped to the waist by sunlight.
And the Fancy? They emerge
from the corners of the eye, low company
from the lie of the land, with guineas
in their stare, without visible means.

The purse is all he fancies. The generations
bunch in his arm.
Toora-li-ooral go the fifes in his blood.
As tall, as straight as a thistle,
Jack Hare squares up to Dancing Jack.

Roger Garfitt

Harvest
(Triolet)

They are mowing wheat
        Through the heavy days;
Through the silent heat
They are mowing wheat;
Flat fields retreat
        Into shrouding haze;
They are mowing wheat
        Through the heavy days.

Frances Cornford

Harvest

A time for hay and a time for harvest
A time for barley and a time for wheat
Shimmering just there in the midst
Of the all sucking heat, the silver sheen
Rippling in the breeze, just there
Over the hedge and behind the trees
Beyond the wide eyed cattle, flicking
Their fly ridden tails, and slobbery tongues.
Comes at last a dusty drone
Giant and subtropical, like an enormous locust
Gorging the corn mechanically
Bolting its food, sick with ladybirds
The golden stream pouring forth
Widgeon, Avalon, Marris Otter,
Huntsman, Galahad and Britannia,
Redstart and Apollo, Marinka and Natasha,
Poacher, Puffin and Dandy.

Carted and augered to fill the silos
Gently copulating with the sky.

While out the back, gleaming half-yellow
In serried ranks, comes the straw
Sullen acres of farmer's corduroy
Undulating and curvaceous
Heaped and humped.
Avenues ignited with a single match.

Racing and rioting, dusk and flames
Burst and burn, red stubble erupting
Inciting arson, dark figures armed
With pitch forks lift the fire here
And place it there, red and smutty
Silhouetted, sheets of flame
Soar and hang, as if the village
Were threatened, about to be burnt

As if vandals had suddenly emerged
From the hedgerows and fired the corn.

The farmer's secret vice.

Damp the shirts
Black the faces
Magnificent the sweat
Eerie the desolation.

James Crowden

Harvest

They were summers full of sunshine. In the fields
we would creep into the stooks of tilted sheaves,
crouching with scratched legs
among the sharp-cut stubble. Tight to dry earth
too low for blades to catch grew speedwell
blue as cornflower, pimpernel
red as poppy.

From two-tined shining forks, long handles worn
to patina by hard palms, the sheaves flew high
onto carts lead-red and blue-sky painted.
The wheels rolled heavy-hubbed and iron-rimmed
weightily field to stack and lighter back again
between straw-littered hedges dull with dust.

As the day drooped to evening we'd ride the wide backs
of Boxer or Diamond to the farmyard. Freed from shafts,
greasy black straps swinging, they could wade
into the pond, drink, bend their great necks.
It was the men's joke not to lift us down
but thwack the chestnut rumps, send us to balance
above the surface smeared with sap-green weed.

They teased us, town children, made us brave;
and I remember them, the faces, names, speech,
working clothes and movements of those men,
the perks they carried home; skimmed milk in cans,
field cabbages in sacks, soft rabbits
swinging head-down from loops of twine, to feed
long families of uncombed dusty children
who stood at laneside gates,
watched us without a smile.

Pamela Gillilan

Harvest at Mynachlog

At last the women come with baskets,
The older one in flowered apron,
A daisied cloth covering the bread
And dappled china, sweet tea
In a vast can. The women stoop
Spreading their cups in the clover.

The engines stop. A buzzard watches
From the fence. We bury our wounds
In the deep grass: sunburnt shoulders,
Bodies scratched with straw, wrists bruised
From the weight of the bales, blood beating.

For hours the baler has been moulding
Golden bricks from the spread straw,
Spewing them at random in the stubble.
I followed the slow load, heaved each
Hot burden, feeling the sun contained.

And unseen over me a man leaned,
Taking the weight to make the toppling
Load. Then the women came, friendly
And cool as patches of flowers at the far
Field edge, mothy and blurred in the heat.

We are soon recovered and roll over
In the grass to take our tea. We talk
Of other harvests. They remember
How a boy, flying his plane so low
Over the cut fields that his father

Straightened from his work to wave his hat
At the boasting sky, died minutes later
On an English cliff, in such a year
As this, the barns brimming gold.

We are quiet again, holding our cups
In turn for the tilting milk, sad, hearing
The sun roar like a rush of grain
Engulfing all winged things that live
One moment in the eclipsing light.

Gillian Clarke

Harvest Hymn

We spray the fields and scatter
  The poison on the ground
So that no wicked wild flowers
  Upon our farm be found.
We like whatever helps us
  To line our purse with pence;
The twenty-four-hour broiler-house
  And neat electric fence.

All concrete sheds around us
  And Jaguars in the yard,
The telly lounge and deep-freeze
  Are ours from working hard.

We fire the fields for harvest,
  The hedges swell the flame,
The oak trees and the cottages
  From which our fathers came.
We give no compensation,
  The earth is ours today,
And if we lose on arable,
  The bungalows will pay.

All concrete sheds around us
  And Jaguars in the yard,
The telly lounge and deep-freeze
  Are ours from working hard.

John Betjeman

Hay

Seven hold their breath,
their full arms itch with gleanings.
In the shadow of their hats
their patient faces hurt.

Under the weight of the sky
three horses hang their heads
at the slackened harness,
her hand tense on the bridle.

Not a cloud sails on,
not a leaf stirs. No
movement of air
in the long grass.

Only the skin of a horse
that shivers off the flies,
and the flick of an ear
will tell they lived: only their absences,

blurred flank, a rubbed-out ear,
the photographer in his black hood,
show still like negatives, in every field
where hay was cut.

Gillian Clarke

Haymaking

After night's thunder far away had rolled
The fiery day had a kernel sweet of cold,
And in the perfect blue the clouds uncurled,
Like the first gods before they made the world
And misery, swimming the stormless sea
In beauty and in divine gaiety.
The smooth white empty road was lightly strewn
With leaves—the holly's Autumn falls in June—
And fir cones standing up stiff in the heat.
The mill-foot water tumbled white and lit
With tossing crystals, happier than any crowd
Of children pouring out of school aloud.
And in the little thickets where a sleeper
For ever might lie lost, the nettle creeper
And garden-warbler sang unceasingly;
While over them shrill shrieked in his fierce glee
The swift with wings and tail as sharp and narrow
As if the bow had flown off with the arrow.
Only the scent of woodbine and hay new mown
Travelled the road. In the field sloping down,
Park-like, to where its willows showed the brook,
Haymakers rested. The tosser lay forsook

Out in the sun; and the long waggon stood
Without its team: it seemed it never would
Move from the shadow of that single yew.
The team, as still, until their task was due,
Beside the labourers enjoyed the shade
That three squat oaks mid-field together made
Upon a circle of grass and weed uncut,
And on the hollow, once a chalk pit, but
Now brimmed with nut and elder-flower so clean.
The men leaned on their rakes, about to begin,
But still. And all were silent. All was old,
This morning time, with a great age untold,
Older than Clare and Cobbett, Morland and Crome,
Than, at the field's far edge, the farmer's home,
A white house crouched at the foot of a great tree.
Under the heavens that know not what years be
The men, the beasts, the trees, the implements
Uttered even what they will in times far hence—
All of us gone out of the reach of change—
Immortal in a picture of an old grange.

Edward Thomas

Hertfordshire

I had forgotten Hertfordshire,
  The large unwelcome fields of roots
Where with my knickerbockered sire
  I trudged in syndicated shoots;

And that unlucky day when I
  Fired by mistake into the ground
Under a Lionel Edwards sky
  And felt disapprobation round.

The slow drive home by motor-car,
　A heavy Rover Landaulette,
Through Welwyn, Hatfield, Potters Bar,
　Tweed and cigar smoke, gloom and wet:

"How many times must I explain
　The way a boy should hold a gun?"
I recollect my father's pain
　At such a milksop for a son.

And now I see these fields once more
　Clothed, thank the Lord, in summer green,
Pale corn waves rippling to a shore
　The shadowy cliffs of elm between,

Colour-washed cottages reed-thatched
　And weather-boarded water mills,
Flint churches, brick and plaster patched,
　On mildly undistinguished hills—

They still are there. But now the shire
　Suffers a devastating change,
Its gentle landscape strung with wire,
　Old places looking ill and strange.

One can't be sure where London ends,
　New towns have filled the fields of root
Where father and his business friends
　Drove in the Landaulette to shoot;

Tall concrete standards line the lane,
　Brick boxes glitter in the sun:
Far more would these have caused him pain
　Than my mishandling of a gun.

　　　　　　　　　John Betjeman

The Hill Field

Look there! What a wheaten
Half-loaf, halfway to bread,
A cornfield is, that is eaten
Away, and harvested:

How like a loaf, where the knife
Has cut and come again,
Jagged where the farmer's wife
Has served the farmer's men,

That steep field is, where the reaping
Has only just begun
On a wedge-shaped front, and the creeping
Steel edges glint in the sun.

See the cheese-like shape it is taking,
The sliced-off walls of the wheat
And the cheese-mite reapers making
Inroads there, in the heat?

It is Breughel or Samuel Palmer,
Some painter, coming between
My eye and the truth of a farmer,
So massively sculpts the scene.

The sickles of poets dazzle
These eyes that were filmed from birth;
And the miller comes with an easel
To grind the fruits of earth.

Donald Davie

Home-Field

But ah! the long gone happy hours
  Of sunny days, in summer-tide,
In home-field bright with shining flow'rs,
  Or sweet with new-mown grass, half-dried;
Where voices laugh'd at merry words,
Below the songs of many birds,
  As slid the time away,
In tree shades wheeling round so slow
That they to me seem'd not to go,
  But linger at a stay.

But now, as I by night come through
  The lonely field with thoughts of day,
The cows lie sleeping in the lew,
  Where then our friends were young and gay;
And cooler winds now scatter down
The elm leaves, faded into brown,
  As slides the hour away,
Where moon cast tree shades wheel so slow,
That they to me seem not to go,
  But linger at a stay.

There seems but little change to me
  In field or path where'er I roam;
The change is where I miss to see
  The life that lived in this old home.
At yonder house, no sun or fire
Shines now on its old dame or sire,
  Whose time is pass'd away;
And yet to us who linger on,
It seems as if it had not gone,
  But this were still their day.

William Barnes

Home-thoughts, from Abroad

O to be in England
Now that April's there,
And whoever wakes in England
Sees, some morning, unaware,
That the lowest boughs and the brushwood sheaf
Round the elm-tree bole are in tiny leaf,
While the chaffinch sings on the orchard bough
In England—now!

And after April, when May follows,
And the whitethroat builds, and all the swallows!
Hark, where my blossomed pear-tree in the hedge
Leans to the field and scatters on the clover
Blossoms and dewdrops—at the bent spray's edge—
That's the wise thrush; he sings each song twice over,
Lest you should think he never could recapture
The first fine careless rapture!
And though the fields look rough with hoary dew,
All will be gay when noontide wakes anew
The buttercups, the little children's dower
—Far brighter than this gaudy melon-flower!

Robert Browning

Horses

When I was a boy here,
traveling the fields for pleasure,
the farms were worked with teams.
As late as then a teamster
was thought an accomplished man,
his art an essential discipline.
A boy learned it by delight
as he learned to use

his body, following the example
of men. The reins of a team
were put into my hands
when I thought the work was play.
And in the corrective gaze
of men now dead I learned
to flesh my will in power
great enough to kill me
should I let it turn.
I learned the other tongue
by which men spoke to beasts
—all its terms and tones.
And by the time I learned,
new ways had changed the time.

The tractors came. The horses
stood in the fields, keepsakes,
grew old, and died. Or were sold
as dogmeat. Our minds received
the revolution of engines, our will
stretched toward the numb endurance
of metal. And that old speech
by which we magnified
our flesh in other flesh
fell dead in our mouths.
The songs of the world died
in our ears as we went within
the uproar of the long syllable
of the motors. Our intent entered
the world as combustion.
Like our travels, our workdays
burned upon the world,
lifting its inwards up
in fire. Veiled in that power
our minds gave up the endless
cycle of growth and decay
and took the unreturning way,
the breathless distance of iron.

But that work, empowered by burning
the world's body, showed us
finally the world's limits
and our own. We had then
the life of a candle, no longer
the ever-returning song
among the grassblades and the leaves.

Did I never forget?
Or did I, after years,
remember? To hear that song
again, though brokenly
in the distances of memory,
is coming home. I came to
a farm, some of it unreachable
by machines, as some of the world
will always be. And so
I came to a team, a pair
of mares—sorrels, with white
tails and manes, beautiful!—
to keep my sloping fields.
Going behind them, the reins
tight over their backs as they stepped
their long strides, revived
again on my tongue the cries
of dead men in the living
fields. Now every move
answers what is still.
This work of love rhymes
living and dead. A dance
is what this plodding is.
A song, whatever is said.

Wendell Berry

Hunting Pheasants in a Cornfield

I

What is so strange about a tree alone in an open field?
It is a willow tree. I walk around and around it.
The body is strangely torn, and cannot leave it.
At last I sit down beneath it.

II

It is a willow tree alone in acres of dry corn.
Its leaves are scattered around its trunk, and around me,
Brown now, and speckled with delicate black.
Only the cornstalks now can make a noise.

III

The sun is cold, burning through the frosty distances of space.
The weeds are frozen to death long ago.
Why then do I love to watch
The sun moving on the chill skin of the branches?

IV

The mind has shed leaves alone for years.
It stands apart with small creatures near its roots.
I am happy in this ancient place,
A spot easily caught sight of above the corn,
If I were a young animal ready to turn home at dusk.

Robert Bly

I Got Two Vields

I got two vields, an' I don't ceäre
What squire mid have a bigger sheäre.
My little zummer-leäze do stratch
All down the hangen, to a patch
O' meäd between a hedge an' rank
Ov elems, an' a river bank.
Where yollow clotes, in spreaden beds
O' floaten leaves, do lift their heads
By benden bulrushes an'zedge
A-swaÿen at the water's edge,
Below the withy that do spread
Athirt the brook his grey-leav'd head.
An' eltrot flowers, milky white,
Do catch the slanten evenen light;
An' in the meäple boughs, along
The hedge, do ring the blackbird's zong;
Or in the day, a-vlee-en drough
The leafy trees, the whoa'se gookoo
Do zing to mowers that do zet
Their zives on end, an' stan' to whet.
From my wold house among the trees
A leäne do goo along the leäze
O' yollow gravel, down between
Two mossy banks vor ever green.
An' trees, a-hangen overhead,
Do hide a trinklen gully-bed,
A-cover'd by a bridge vor hoss
Or man a-voot to come across.
Zoo wi' my hwomestead, I don't ceäre
What squire mid have a bigger sheäre!

William Barnes

'I grant indeed that fields and flocks have charms'

I grant indeed that fields and flocks have charms
For him that grazes or for him that farms;
But when amid such pleasing scenes I trace
The poor laborious natives of the place,
And see the mid-day sun, with fervid ray,
On their bare heads and dewy temples play;
While some, with feebler heads and fainter hearts,
Deplore their fortune, yet sustain their parts:
Then shall I dare these real ills to hide
In tinsel trappings of poetic pride?

George Crabbe
from The Village, Book II

'In a summer season when the sun was mild'

In a summer season when the sun was mild
I clad myself in clothes as I'd become a sheep;
In the habit of a hermit unholy of works
Walked wide in this world, watching for wonders.
And on a May morning, on Malvern Hills,
There befell me as by magic a marvelous thing:
I was weary of wandering and went to rest
At the bottom of a broad bank by a brook's side,
And as I lay lazily looking in the water
I slipped into a slumber, it sounded so pleasant.
There came to me reclining there a most curious dream
That I was in a wilderness, nowhere that I knew;
But as I looked into the east, up high toward the sun,
I saw a tower on a hill-top, trimly built,
A deep dale beneath, a dungeon tower in it,
With ditches deep and dark and dreadful to look at.
A fair field full of folk I found between them,
Of human beings of all sorts, the high and the low,
Working and wandering as the world requires.

Some applied themselves to plowing, played very rarely,
Sowing seeds and setting plants worked very hard:
Won what wasters gluttonously consume.
And some pursued pride, put on proud clothing,
Came all got up in garments garish to see.
To prayers and penance many put themselves,
All for love of our Lord lived hard lives,
Hoping thereafter to have Heaven's bliss—
Such as hermits and anchorites that hold to their cells,
Don't care to go cavorting about the countryside,
With some lush livelihood delighting their bodies.
And some made themselves merchants—they managed better,
As it seems to our sight that such men prosper.
And some make mirth as minstrels can
And get gold for their music, guiltless, I think.
But jokers and word jugglers, Judas' children,
Invent fantasies to tell about and make fools of themselves,
And have whatever wits they need to work if they wanted.

William Langland
from The Vision of Piers Plowman
(translated by E. Talbot Donaldson)

In December

In December the stubble nearly is
Most loved of things.
The rooks as in the dark trees are its friends
And make part of it . . .

Now when the hills shine far
And light and set off
That darkness, all my heart cries angrily
That music to fashion

For if not so, one must go
To the stubble every day
For comfort against such emptiness
As lost treasures make.

Cruelly scare the choughs from
Fallows and trees alike—
Though dim in love, or bright far
With the hills heroically they ally.

Ivor Gurney

'In early spring, when the ice on the snowy mountains'

In early spring, when the ice on the snowy mountains
Melts and the west wind loosens and crumbles the clods,
Then it's high time for my bull at the deep-driven plough
To groan, and the share to gleam with the furrow's polishing.
That field and that alone
Answers the prayer of the demanding farmer
Which twice has felt the sun and twice the cold;
Its superabundant harvests burst his barns.
But with untried land, before we cleave it with iron,
We must con its varying moods of wind and sky
With care—the place's native style and habit,
What crops the region will bear and what refuse.
Here corn will prosper better, there the grape,
Elsewhere young trees or greenery unbidden.
Look how Tmolus sends us its fragrant saffron,
India ivory, incense the soft Sabaeans,
But iron the naked Chalybes, Pontus the pungent
Musk, and Epirus mares for Olympic palms.
Nature imposed these everlasting covenants
From the first on certain regions, right from the time
When Deucalion over the empty spaces of earth
Cast those stones that produced the race of men—
A hard race. Up then, and if your soil is rich,
From the first months of the year let your stout bulls
Turn it over, and let the clods lie there
For dusty summer to bake with ripening suns;

But if your soil is poor, it will be enough
To furrow it lightly just as Arcturus is rising—
There, lest the flourishing crop be choked with weeds,
Here, lest the meagre moisture dry to a desert.
    Harvested land in alternating fallow
You will let recover, crusting in idleness;
Or at another season sow with spelt
Fields you have stripped of beans with quivering pods,
Rich beans or slender vetch or bitter lupine
With its brittle haulm and rustling undergrowth.
True, flax can parch, and oats can parch, and poppies
Steeped in Lethaean slumber parch the earth;
Still, alternation's no great labour: only
Don't be ashamed to saturate dry soil
With rich manure, and scatter grimy ashes
Over exhausted ground.
Thus too by change of crops, fields can be rested
Without the thanklessness of untilled land.
Again, it often pays, when fields are cropless,
To fire the stubble with rapidly crackling flames—
Whether it is that hence the soil derives
Mysterious strength and nourishing enrichment;
Or that the fire burns out all noxiousness
And sweats out surplus moisture; or that the heat
Opens new paths and loosens hidden pores
To let the seedlings drink; or tightens rather
And closes gaping ducts, lest seeping rains
Or power of parching sun too fierce, or cold,
The north wind's penetrating cold, may blast them.
He greatly helps his land who takes a mattock
To break the sluggish clods, and drags bush-harrows—
Ceres looks down from heaven and rewards him—
He too who, having first upheaved the surface
In ridges, breaks them down with angled ploughshare,
And disciplines the acres he commands.

Virgil
from The Georgics, Book I
(translated by L. P. Wilkinson)

In Flanders Fields

In Flanders fields the poppies blow
Between the crosses, row on row,
    That mark our place; and in the sky
    The larks, still bravely singing, fly
Scarce heard amid the guns below.

We are the Dead. Short days ago
We lived, felt dawn, saw sunset glow,
    Loved and were loved, and now we lie
    In Flanders fields.

Take up our quarrel with the foe:
To you from failing hands we throw
    The torch; be yours to hold it high.
    If ye break faith with us who die
We shall not sleep, though poppies grow
      In Flanders fields.

John McCrae

In Summer

Night lies down
in the field when the moon
leaves. Head in clover,
held still.

It is brief,
this time of darkness,
hands of night
loosefisted, long hair
outspread.

Sooner than one would dream,
the first bird
wakes with a sobbing cry. Whitely

dew begins to drift
cloudily.
Leafily naked, forms of the world
are revealed,
all asleep. Colors

come slowly
up from behind the hilltop,
looking for forms to fill for the day,
dwellings.
Night
must rise and
move on, stiff and
not yet awake.

Denise Levertov

'In that open field'

In that open field
If you do not come too close, if you do not come too close,
On a summer midnight, you can hear the music
Of the weak pipe and the little drum
And see them dancing around the bonfire
The association of man and woman
In daunsinge, signifying matrimonie—
A dignified and commodiois sacrament.
Two and two, necessarye coniunction,
Holding eche other by the hand or the arm
Whiche betokeneth concorde. Round and round the fire
Leaping through the flames, or joined in circles,
Rustically solemn or in rustic laughter

Lifting heavy feet in clumsy shoes,
Earth feet, loam feet, lifted in country mirth
Mirth of those long since under earth
Nourishing the corn. Keeping time,
Keeping the rhythm in their dancing
As in their living in the living seasons
The time of the seasons and the constellations
The time of milking and the time of harvest
The time of the coupling of man and woman
And that of beasts. Feet rising and falling.
Eating and drinking. Dung and death.

    Dawn points, and another day
Prepares for heat and silence. Out at sea the dawn wind
Wrinkles and slides. I am here
Or there, or elsewhere. In my beginning.

T. S. Eliot
from 'East Coker'

In the Fallow Field

I went down on my hands and knees
Looking for trees,
Twin leaves that, sprung from seeds,
Were now too big
For stems much thinner than a twig.
These soon with chamomile and clover
And other fallow weeds
Would be turned over;
And I was thinking how
It was a pity someone should not know
That a great forest fell before the plough.

Andrew Young

In the Fields

Lord, when I look at lovely things which pass,
    Under old trees the shadows of young leaves
Dancing to please the wind along the grass,
    Or the gold stillness of the August sun on the August sheaves;
Can I believe there is a heavenlier world than this?
    And if there is
Will the strange heart of any everlasting thing
    Bring me these dreams that take my breath away?
They come at evening with the home-flying rooks and the scent of hay,
    Over the fields. They come in Spring.

Charlotte Mew

The Invisible Globe

On bare hillsides, pale fields,
History was a story indeed,
Of labour and conflict
And prayer; now remote
Like a stranger's dream.

Labourer, monk,
Each singular one:
They have abandoned the place
To contemplation;
The cloisters have merged
In silence deeper than prayer.

But to the chalk there is
One human fact in the landscape
The landscape can share:
All the dead
Contract to a single bone.

Chalk, too, has its dream.
Of the bone
On a white ground
Of endless beginnings.

Jeremy Hooker

John Barleycorn

There were three men came out of the west
Their fortunes for to try,
And these three men made a solemn vow
John Barleycorn should die.

They've ploughed, they've sown, they've harrowed him in,
Throw'd clods upon his head,
And these three men made a solemn vow
John Barleycorn was dead.

They've let him lie for a very long time
Till the rain from heaven did fall,
Then little Sir John sprung up his head
And soon amazed them all.

They've let him stand till Midsummer Day
Till he looked both pale and wan,
And little Sir John's grown a long, long beard
And so become a man.

They've hired men with their scythes so sharp
To cut him off at the knee,
They've rolled and tied him by the waist,
Serving him most barb'rously.

They've hired men with their sharp pitch forks
Who pricked him to the heart,
And the loader he served him worse than that
For he's bound him to the cart.

They've wheeled him round and around the field
Till they came unto the barn
And there they've made a solemn mow
Of poor John Barleycorn.

They've hired men with the crabtree sticks
To cut him skin from bone,
And the miller he has served him worse than that
For he's ground him between two stones.

Here's little Sir John in the nut brown bowl
And here's brandy in the glass,
And little Sir John in the nut brown bowl
Proved the strongest man at last

For the huntsman he can't hunt the fox
And so loudly blow his horn
And the tinker he can't mend kettles nor pots
Without a little barleycorn.

Traditional

The Land

('Friendly Brook'—A Diversity of Creatures)

When Julius Fabricius, Sub-Prefect of the Weald,
In the days of Diocletian owned our Lower River-field,
He called to him Hobdenius—a Briton of the Clay,
Saying: "What about that River-piece for layin' in to hay?"

And the aged Hobden answered: "I remember as a lad
My father told your father that she wanted dreenin' bad.
An' the more that you neglect her the less you'll get her clean,
Have it jest *as* you've a mind to, but, if I was you, I'd dreen."

So they drained it long and crossways in the lavish Roman style—
Still we find among the river-drift their flakes of ancient tile,
And in drouthy middle August, when the bones of meadows show,
We can trace the lines they followed sixteen hundred years ago.

Then Julius Fabricius died as even Prefects do,
And after certain centuries, Imperial Rome died too.
Then did robbers enter Britain from across the Northern main
And our Lower River-field was won by Ogier the Dane.

Well could Ogier work his war-boat—well could Ogier wield his
    brand—
Much he knew of foaming waters—not so much of farming land.
So he called to him a Hobden of the old unaltered blood,
Saying: "What about that River-bit; she doesn't look no good?"

And the aged Hobden answered: " 'Tain't for *me* to interfere,
But I've known that bit o' meadow now for five and fifty year.
Have it *jest* as you've a mind to, but I've proved it time on time,
If you want to change her nature you have *got* to give her lime!"

Ogier sent his wains to Lewes, twenty hours' solemn walk,
And drew back great abundance of the cool, grey, healing chalk.
And old Hobden spread it broadest, never heeding what was in't.—
Which is why in cleaning ditches, now and then we find a flint.

Ogier died. His sons grew English—Anglo-Saxon was their name—
Till out of blossomed Normandy another pirate came;
For Duke William conquered England and divided with his men,
And our lower River-field he gave to William of Warenne.

But the Brook (you know her habit) rose one rainy Autumn night
And tore down sodden flitches of the bank to left and right.
So, said William to his Bailiff as they rode their dripping rounds:
"Hob, what about that River-bit—the Brook's got up no bounds?"

And that aged Hobden answered: " 'Tain't my business to advise,
But ye might ha' known 'twould happen from the way the valley
    lies.
Where ye can't hold back the water you must try and save the sile.
Hev it jest as you've a *mind* to, but if I was you, I'd spile!"

They spiled along the water-course with trunks of willow-trees,
And planks of elms behind 'em and immortal oaken knees.
And when the spates of Autumn whirl the gravel-beds away
You can see their faithful fragments, iron-hard in iron clay.

Georgii Quinti Anno Sexto, I, who own the River-field,
Am fortified with title-deeds, attested, signed and sealed,
Guaranteeing me, my assigns, my executors and heirs
All sorts of powers and profits which—are neither mine nor theirs.

I have rights of chase and warren, as my dignity requires.
I can fish—but Hobden tickles. I can shoot—but Hobden wires.
I repair, but he reopens, certain gaps which, men allege,
Have been used by every Hobden since a Hobden swapped a hedge.

Shall I dog his morning progress o'er the track-betraying dew?
Demand his dinner-basket into which my pheasant flew?
Confiscate his evening faggot into which the conies ran,
And summons him to judgment? I would sooner summons Pan.

His dead are in the churchyard—thirty generations laid.
Their names went down in Domesday Book when Domesday
    Book was made;
And the passion and the piety and prowess of his line
Have seeded, rooted, fruited in some land the Law calls mine.

Not for any beast that burrows, not for any bird that flies,
Would I lose his large sound counsel, miss his keen amending eyes.
He is bailiff, woodman, wheelwright, field-surveyor, engineer,
And if flagrantly a poacher—'tain't for me to interfere.

"Hob, what about the River-bit?" I turn to him again,
With Fabricius and Ogier and William of Warenne.
"Hev it jest as you've a mind to, *but*"—and so he takes
    command.
For whoever pays the taxes old Mus' Hobden owns the land.

Rudyard Kipling

The Licorice Fields at Pontefract

In the licorice fields at Pontefract
      My love and I did meet
And many a burdened licorice bush
      Was blooming round our feet;
Red hair she had and golden skin,
Her sulky lips were shaped for sin,
Her sturdy legs were flannel-slack'd,
The strongest legs in Pontefract.

The light and dangling licorice flowers
      Gave off the sweetest smells;
From various black Victorian towers
      The Sunday evening bells
Came pealing over dales and hills

And tanneries and silent mills
And lowly streets where country stops
And little shuttered corner shops.

She cast her blazing eyes on me
    And plucked a licorice leaf;
I was her captive slave and she
    My red-haired robber chief.
Oh love! for love I could not speak,
It left me winded, wilting, weak
And held in brown arms strong and bare
And wound with flaming ropes of hair.

John Betjeman

Linum

It is not tall enough, it will not make a crop—
it has changed its name. It used to be flax,
maker of sheets for fine ladies' beds.
Now it is linseed; feeds cattle.
It is high as a knee, blown with threads of leaf,
scattered with flower. What corn is blue?
They are mouths, they are stars, they gleam sweet
as those pictures of children under dark leaf
in frames of deep gilt. It knows nothing;
the sky is bitterer. Last night's sun
was icy lemon, with drifts of grey;
the morning's blaze is for storm. The flax flowers
begin to shimmer, with a metal edge,
to reflect ripe cloud, race a colder sea.
The flies still whirl in hot air, and I
rise quick up the ridge, through the brief, starred fields.
It is not every day you can run through the sky.

Alison Brackenbury

Lost Acres

These acres, always again lost
    By every new ordnance-survey
And searched for at exhausting cost
    Of time and thought, are still away.

They have their paper-substitute—
    Intercalation of an inch
At the so-many-thousandth foot—
    And no one parish feels the pinch.

But lost they are, despite all care,
    And perhaps likely to be bound
Together in a piece somewhere,
    A plot of undiscovered ground.

Invisible, they have the spite
    To swerve the tautest measuring-chain
And the exact theodolite
    Perched every side of them in vain.

Yet, be assured, we have no need
    To plot these acres of the mind
With prehistoric fern and reed
    And monsters such as heroes find.

Maybe they have their flowers, their birds,
    Their trees behind the phantom fence,
But of a substance without words:
    To walk there would be loss of sense.

Robert Graves

The Mare

The mare lies down in the grass where the nest of the skylark
    is hidden.
Her eyes drink the delicate horizon moving behind the song.
Deep sink the skies, a well of voices. Her sleep is the vessel
    of Summer.
That climbing music requires the hidden music at rest.

Her body is utterly given to the light, surrendered in perfect
    abandon
To the heaven above her shadow, still as her first-born day.
Softly the wind runs over her. Circling the meadow, her hooves
Rest in a race of daisies, halted where butterflies stand.

Do not pass her too close. It is easy to break the circle
And lose that indolent fullness rounded under the ray
Falling on light-eared grasses your footstep must not yet wake.
It is easy to darken the sun of her unborn foal at play.

Vernon Watkins

Meadow in Drought

There was still shade on the old path
to Brongynnes meadow, but no softness,
no coolness, no untarnished green,
no dampness to slake the cravings
of this exigent summer.
Sheep had passed along, eating the leaves
off willow-herb and fern, stretching
on teetering hind-hooves to try
birch, hazel, oak. They had broken down
the generous shapes of foliage
to maimed and ominous skeletons, akin
to the hostile saplessness of grass.

The gate's rough wood was hot to touch.
Beyond in the yellowed meadow
a wind like the moving spirit of heat
flattened harebells, shrivelled red-leaved sorrel.
Under browning oaks by the shrunken river
stood a boy and girl, looking with love
at the meadow whose parched and dying beauty
they saw green, springing, with their own
fertile unfearing happiness;
and gathered to them, against dry years,
the soft-leaved hour, the valley of abundance.

Ruth Bidgood

To Meddowes

Ye have been fresh and green,
    Ye have been fill'd with flowers:
And ye the Walks have been
    Where Maids have spent their houres.

You have beheld how they
    With *Wicker Arks* did come
To kisse, and beare away
    The richer Couslips home.

Y'ave heard them sweetly sing,
    And seen them in a Round:
Each Virgin, like a Spring,
    With Hony-succles crown'd.

But now, we see, none here,
    Whose silv'rie feet did tread,
And with dishevell'd Haire,
    Adorn'd this smoother Mead.

Like Unthrifts, having spent,
   Your stock, and needy grown,
Y'are left here to lament
   Your poore estates, alone.

Robert Herrick

Millom Cricket Field

The soft mouths of summer bite at the eyes,
Toothless as a rose and red as the ragged robin;
     Mouths on lip
     Rouse to sleep
And the green of the field reflected in the skies.

The elder-flower curls inward to a dream,
And memories swarm as a halo of midges;
   Children on the grass,
   Wicket-high, pass,
In blue sailor jackets and jerseys brown and cream.

Among the champion, legendary men
I see my childhood roll like a cricket-ball.
   To watch that boy
   Is now my joy—
That he could watch me not was his joy then.

Norman Nicholson

The Mores

Far spread the moorey ground a level scene
Bespread with rush and one eternal green
That never felt the rage of blundering plough
Though centurys wreathed springs blossoms on its brow
Still meeting plains that stretched them far away
In uncheckt shadows of green brown and grey
Unbounded freedom ruled the wandering scene
Nor fence of ownership crept in between
To hide the prospect of the following eye
Its only bondage was the circling sky
One mighty flat undwarfed by bush and tree
Spread its faint shadow of immensity
And lost itself which seemed to eke its bounds
In the blue mist the orisons edge surrounds

Now this sweet vision of my boyish hours
Free as spring clouds and wild as summer flowers
Is faded all—a hope that blossomed free
And hath been once no more shall ever be
Inclosure came and trampled on the grave
Of labours rights and left the poor a slave
And memorys pride ere want to wealth did bow
Is both the shadow and the substance now
The sheep and cows were free to range as then
Where change might prompt nor felt the bonds of men
Cows went and came with evening morn and night
To the wild pasture as their common right
And sheep unfolded with the rising sun
Heard the swains shout and felt their freedom won
Tracked the red fallow field and heath and plain
Then met the brook and drank and roamed again
The brook that dribbled on as clear as glass
Beneath the roots they hid among the grass
While the glad shepherd traced their tracks along
Free as the lark and happy as her song
But now alls fled and flats of many a dye
That seemed to lengthen with the following eye

Moors loosing from the sight far smooth and blea
Where swopt the plover in its pleasure free
Are vanished now with commons wild and gay
As poets visions of lifes early day
Mulberry bushes where the boy would run
To fill his hands with fruit are grubbed and done
And hedgrow briars—flower lovers overjoyed
Came and got flower pots—these are all destroyed
And sky bound mores in mangled garbs are left
Like mighty giants of their limbs bereft
Fence now meets fence in owners little bounds
Of field and meadow large as garden grounds
In little parcels little minds to please
With men and flocks imprisoned ill at ease
Each little path that led its pleasant way
As sweet as morning leading night astray
Where little flowers bloomed round a varied host
That travel felt delighted to be lost
Nor grudged the steps that he had taen as vain
When right roads traced his journeys and again
Nay on a broken tree hed sit awhile
To see the mores and fields and meadows smile
Sometimes with cowslaps smothered—then all white
With daiseys—then the summers splendid sight
Of corn fields crimson oer the 'headach' bloomd
Like splendid armys for the battle plumed
He gazed upon them with wild fancys eye
As fallen landscapes from an evening sky
These paths are stopt—the rude philistines thrall
Is laid upon them and destroyed them all
Each little tyrant with his little sign
Shows where man claims earth glows no more divine
But paths to freedom and to childhood dear
A board sticks up to notice 'no road here'
And on the tree with ivy overhung
The hated sign by vulgar taste is hung
As tho the very birds should learn to know
When they go there they must no further go

This with the poor scared freedom bade good bye
And much they feel it in the smothered sigh
And birds and trees and flowers without a name
All sighed when lawless laws enclosure came
And dreams of plunder in such rebel schemes
Have found too truly that they were but dreams

John Clare

Mowing

There was never a sound beside the wood but one,
And that was my long scythe whispering to the ground.
What was it it whispered? I knew not well myself;
Perhaps it was something about the heat of the sun,
Something, perhaps, about the lack of sound—
And that was why it whispered and did not speak.
It was no dream of the gift of idle hours,
Or easy gold at the hand of fay or elf:
Anything more than the truth would have seemed too weak
To the earnest love that laid the swale in rows,
Not without feeble-pointed spikes of flowers
(Pale orchises), and scared a bright green snake.
The fact is the sweetest dream that labor knows.
My long scythe whispered and left the hay to make.

Robert Frost

My Meadow

Well, it's still the loveliest meadow in all Vermont.
I believe that truly, yet for years have hardly

seen it, I think, having lived too long with it—
until I went to clean up the mess of firewood

left by the rural electric co-op when they cut
my clump of soft maples "threatening" their lines,

this morning, the last day of September. My maple leaves
were spilled in the grass, deep crimson, I worked

with axe and chainsaw, and when I was done I sat
on my rock that had housed my fox before the state

executed him on suspicion of rabies, and then
I looked at my meadow. I saw how it lies between

the little road and the little brook, how its borders
are birch and hemlock, popple and elm and ash,

white, green, red, brown, and gray, and how my grass
is composed in smooth serenity. Yet I have hankered

for six years after that meadow I saw in Texas
near Camp Wood because I discovered an armadillo

there and saw two long-tailed flycatchers
at their fantastic mating dance in the air.

Now I saw my meadow. And I called myself all kinds
of a blind Yankee fool—not so much for hankering,

more for the quality of my looking that could make me
see in my mind what I could not see in my meadow.

However, I saw my serviceberry tree at the edge
of the grass where little pied asters, called Farewell-

to-Summer, made a hedge, my serviceberry still limping
from last winter's storms, and I went

and trimmed it. The small waxy pointed leaves
were delicate with the colors of coral and mallow

and the hesitating blush of the sky at dawn.
When I finished I stepped over my old fence

and sat by the brook on moss sodden from last night's
rain and got the seat of my britches wet.

I looked at my brook. It curled over my stones
that looked back at me again with the pathos

of their paleozoic eyes. I thought of my
discontents. The brook, curled in its reflections

of ferns and asters and bright leaves, was whispering
something that made no sense. Then I closed my eyes

and heard my brook inside my head. It told me—
and I saw a distant inner light like the flash

of a waterdrop on a turning leaf—it told me
maybe I have lived too long with the world.

Hayden Carruth

Naming the Field

We here call this *grass*, you can pick it
like this, it is the earth's *hair*, feel *hair*
on your head. Pick a *strand*
of *grass*, one of the earth's *hairs*,
you can whistle through it like this,
you can chew it and, spread out,
it is a kind of *carpet*. This is what we call *rock*

sticking through the *carpet*, the *rock* is not a *strand*
but is *hard*, like my *head*, you see, if I tap it,
but *harder* than *head*. This, flowing through the *field*,
we call *stream*. *Field* is *carpet* between *hedges*
and *stream* divides it. Is this place the end

of your pilgrimage or are you passing only,
have you become astray here? *Hedge*
is what we call this *flowing* upwards of *shrubs* and *bushes*,
of *runners* and *nests*, of parasitic *blooms*. The *field*
in its *flowing* to us through *time*

is named Saint Alphege's, who was beaten to death
with ox *bones*. These, under the skin, we call *bones*,
you see I am thin, my *bones* stick through almost
like *rocks*. This all around us, invisible
we call *air*, see when I *breathe* my *lungs*
fill with *air*. I have had my place here, I wash my *bones*
under my *skin*
in the *stream*, so as to be *clean*
when the *earth* claims me back. This—*splash, splash*—
we call *marsh*. These *reeds* in the *marsh*
are the long thin grave stones
of those who went straight *down*
thrilling to the call of the steep deep,
their *bodies* long thin needles—'This won't hurt,
this won't hurt a bit.' I cannot explain *home*,
it is not *room*, nor is it contained within *stone* walls. The *stream*

is at *home* in *field*, *rocks* are,
air is, *grass* is, *honeysuckle* is—smell it
and *I* am.

David Hart

Neutral

Green grass growing back through a stubble field
with chequered brushstrokes, thistle and chickweed
proliferating, you can feel the change—
the filtering of tiny air-borne seeds

drifting off microcosmically, the tap-
drip in the wood's the tick of poplar leaves
descending, yellow, skate-shaped, ribbed with green.
The air smells of woodsmoke, of hay-blond sheaves,

the magpie lifting's a blue and white fan
rapidly flurrying. I stare inside
a cavernous silo; a transistor
bubbles with its platitudinous tide

of universal misexpenditures,
the East and West, the claptrap of the day,
the tiny marks that don't make history,
the chaff that's either lost or blown away

through man's unregenerate militancy . . .
I cross a field and then another field,
the sky's a grey agate, the distant sea
is the blue-grey of a woodlouse's shield

locked tight into a ball in mute defence.
My footsteps terminate before the sea,
safe, neutral ground overrun by bracken,
the wild unclaimed kestrel's territory.

Jeremy Reed

The New Cemetery

Now that the town's dead
Amount to more than its calculable future,
They are opening a new graveyard

In the three-hedged field where once
Horses of the L.M.S. delivery wagons
Were put to grass. Beside the fence

Of the cricket-ground, we'd watch
On Saturday afternoon, soon after the umpires
Laid the bails to the stumps and the match

Had begun. They'd lead them
Then between railways and St George's precinct—huge
Beasts powerful as the steam

Engines they were auxiliary to:
Hanked muscles oscillating slow and placid as pistons,
Eyes blinkered from all view

Of the half-acre triangle of green,
Inherited for Sunday. But once they'd slipped the harness,
And the pinched field was seen

With its blue lift of freedom,
Those haunches heaved like a sub-continental earthquake
Speeded up in film.

Half a ton of horse-flesh
Rose like a balloon, gambolled like a month-old lamb;
Hind legs lashed

Out at inoffensive air,
Capsized a lorryful of weekdays, stampeded down
Fifty yards of prairie.

We heard the thump
Of hoof on sun-fired clay in the hush between
The bowler's run-up

And the click of the late
Cut. And when, one end-of-season day, they lead me
Up through the churchyard gate

To that same
Now consecrated green—unblinkered and at last delivered
Of a life-time's

Load of parcels—let me fling
My hooves at the boundary wall and bang them down again,
Making the thumped mud ring.

Norman Nicholson

New Crops

O engines
flying over the light, barren
as shuttles, thrown over a huge
woof

crossply
of hedgeless snail tracks,
you are so high,

you've felled the damp crevices
you've felled the boulder-strewn meadow
the lichen
the strong plum tree.

O engines
swaying your rubber batons
on pods, on ripe lupins,
on a chameleon terrace
of greenlessness,

you're withdrawn from a sea
of harvests, you're the foreshore

of soaked soil leaching
undrinkable streams.

Helen Dunmore

No Sprinkling of Bright Weeds

Earth—that old-hat phrase of superseded days—
goes red with my slack-satin flowers,
my poppies; my cornflowers of absolute blue—
both mix into my wheat. Also out of the ears

with which it's level stares each sepal-criss-
crossed flat corncockle eye,
magenta, without a blink the whole
day into the hot sky.

  Lady, not now. Lady in whose gay
bleached hair with ears of wheat with poppies if not corn-
flowers and cockles mixed, and in your south love-
in-the-mist and black-pupilled scarlet pheasant's eye,

Sunburned Ceres, you must understand (you catch my
tone) that now across all plains—no longer fields—
your very carefully treated wheat must be
a clean stand for maximated yields.

Our bodily, of course our economic and our
    advertising needs
permit, Lady, except among peasants backward on thin
    soil,
no sprinkling of bright weeds.

Geoffrey Grigson

Notes on a Field-Map
in memoriam Cash Martineau

Corrugated and clouded,
many acres foxed,
face up in every season.

rookwing to mushroom

The Little Ouse still oozes
through Gallant's Meadow.
Fenced and throttled.

mushroom to muck

Badwell Hill Meadow.
Here I whistled Tempest
down the generous ride.

muck to chestnut

Bales of wild silk.
And the plump does
up-ending into their warrens.

chestnut to straw

Under light's blinding eye
boundaries, features,
characters all faded.

straw to chert

Here is Bull's Croft,
First Beeches. Second . . .
Felled. Gone to ground.

chert to pigeonwing

 ome   ado
This was Home Meadow.
Silver dust.

Kevin Crossley-Holland

O ubi campi!

The soil sandy and the plow light, neither
virgin land nor near by the market town,
cropping one staple without forethought, steer
stedfastly ruinward year in year out,
grudging the labour and cost of manure,
drudging not for gain but fewer dollars loss
yet certain to make a bad bargain by
misjudging the run of prices. How glad
you will be when the state takes your farm for
arrears of taxes! No more cold daybreaks
saffron under the barbed wire the east wind
thrums, nor wet noons, nor starpinned nights! The choir
of gnats is near a full-close. The windward
copse stops muttering inwardly its prose
bucolics. You will find a city job
or relief—or doss-and-grub—resigned to
anything except your own numb toil, the
seasonal plod to spoil the land, alone.

Basil Bunting

The Old Showfield

An aeroplane might still see where
postholes reveal in deeper green
their outline of the ring,
but the parade of champions,
pride reflected in challenge cups,
the hot importance of who won,
have burned to blank white ash,
only scattered scraps remain.

What would I buy with my pocket money?
Would there be Victoria plums?
Could the tent-poles stand the storm?
Why was the dawn so slow to come?

By nine o'clock a spate of livestock,
flowers, produce for the tent,
was funnelling through the gate.
The field rang loud with recognising
distant relations from nearby dales,
"How do?" "How ista?" "What's thi fettle?",
"Champion", "Middlin", "Nut sa bad".
Sometimes sympathy for a family death,
always "Have ya got your hay?",
promises to meet, talk later,
as they hurried on with their exhibits.
But only a step before they stopped
and started it all again
with another face they might not have seen
since last year in the same place.

Canvas hushed our voices
softened the light, enclosed
the mingled scents of gingerbread
sweet peas and woollen rugs
spiced with trodden grass.
Exhibitors loitered after time
to slide their butter to the front,

pick a speck off a pillowslip,
stroke petals into place.

They ran with buckets from the beck
for the final rinse of Herdwick hoar-frost
faces, fly-whisk Shorthorn tails,
before the judges began to open-up mouths,
feel muscle and bone, eye conformation,
consider condition, turn away to consult,
like a morning hospital round.

Grandfather with another bearded
patriarch, both in their eighties
leaning on horn-handled sticks.
Ned Nelson pointed with his pipe
as I stood silent in my new school cap,
"Is this yan o' thine, Jerry?"
"Aye Ned, he's Thomas's lad."
"A see thy neb's still cummin."
And off they went to the sheep pens,
talking dead tups back to life.

Cold meats, pickled beetroot, piccalilli, shallots,
teacakes, rumbutter, new bread and sponge,
Swiss rolls and fruit loaf, tomatoes and tongue,
were lined up on tables the length of the schoolroom,
free lunch for helpers, committee, and judges.
High on the wall, 'John Cabot receiving his charter'
saw Mrs W pouring out tea, Mrs R washing up
while Mrs B was filling fresh plates,
remembered them all down there at desks
doing their sums on squeaky slates.

The landlord of 'The Shepherds' Arms'
was generous, and wasn't,
when he gave the show-field free.
His pub was just outside the gate,
a special licence made his year's rent
on that one Wednesday.

Men's hands grew blue from the pass-out stamp,
their faces reddened, voices swelled
arguing which gimmer twinter, shepherd's bitch,
mangold wurzel, Clydesdale mare, whatever,
would have won with a sighted judge.

When the tent had gone,
when we'd sent posts and pens
trestles and tables into store,
we could read the tracks,
take-off divots at the jumps,
the marquee's roundabout bruise,
a puddled lane where punters' feet
had gone from board to board.
Sometimes a shilling glinted there.

We pouched the day, like hamsters,
brought out the words of what we'd heard,
who'd been, and who had not been there,
chewed them again in the Co-op store,
Cockermouth Auction, Whitehaven Market,
till the whole county knew
what had gone on at Ennerdale Show.

Tom Rawling

On Merrow Down

This is the moment of the cuckoo bee,
lurching from bullace to cardamine;
heat bleeds the trees; Brimstone and Orange Tip
wink in the plaited grass; the meadow stands
in the pool of its own shade, summer-stunned,
even the dowsing beetle, on a spiked
acre of Yorkshire Fog, is heron-like,
wading in fleece; stopped rabbits dream of air,

pressed to their pulsing young, terrified, live
scent maps of fox paths and snares;
the little owl waits in the lucid roof,
above the lunchtime walkers, to descend
through the cool stratus of an evening wind
into the hoop of rain and yellow stars.

John Burnside
from An English Suite

On the Grasshopper and Cricket

The poetry of earth is never dead:
  When all the birds are faint with the hot sun,
  And hide in cooling trees, a voice will run
From hedge to hedge about the new-mown mead;
That is the Grasshopper's—he takes the lead
  In summer luxury,—he has never done
  With his delights; for when tired out with fun
He rests at ease beneath some pleasant weed.
The poetry of earth is ceasing never:
  On a lone winter evening, when the frost
    Has wrought a silence, from the stove there shrills
The Cricket's song, in warmth increasing ever,
  And seems to one in drowsiness half lost,
    The Grasshopper's among some grassy hills.

John Keats

On the Hill

One, two, three, four—eleven,
  Slowly the church clock beat;
I laughed knowing the slope of heaven
  Rolled around my feet.

A thousand flowers were there,
  Rock-rose and tormentil,
Blue rampion that claws the air
  And rubied pimpernel;

Great downy-leaved mullein
  Tall as a man can walk,
Heavy with blobs of gold that climb
  Blossoming his thick stalk;

Rest-harrow, sage, self-heal,
  Eyebright, squinancy-wort,
Marjoram that grows too tall
  And thyme that grows too short.

God, as these grasses are,
  (I prayed there) so be I;
For them no sad presaging star
  Darkens a flawless sky.

Of death they have no heed;
  Fruitfully they die,
Coining in dead living seed
  Their immortality.

Andrew Young

Over the Fields

Whoever heard of a seamless garment?
This is a sky scabby with stars,
a moon that eats a hole in the grass,
a night announced by the drone of a plane
and lit by tail lights.

There's owl screech and fox-bark,
wake them and the geese will laugh
blisters to your face.
But the phone still rings,
the television flickers,
over the fields wires hum.

Maura Dooley

Pasturelands

We scurry over the pastures
chasing the windstrewn oak-leaves.

We kiss
the fresh petals of cowslips and primroses.

We discover frog-spawn in the wet ditch.

Herbert Read

Pied Beauty

Glory be to God for dappled things—
    For skies of couple-colour as a brinded cow;
      For rose-moles all in stipple upon trout that swim;
Fresh-firecoal chestnut-falls; finches' wings;
    Landscape plotted and pieced—fold, fallow, and plough;
      And all trades, their gear and tackle and trim.

All things counter, original, spare, strange;
    Whatever is fickle, freckled (who knows how?)
      With swift, slow; sweet, sour; adazzle, dim;
He fathers-forth whose beauty is past change:
                      Praise him.

Gerard Manley Hopkins

Ploughing

The tractor-driver ploughs his road as straight as a
    Roman's,
Changing rough stubble into smooth, shining earth,
Turning it over in waves that break and fall motionless.

A white pennant of gulls follows, shrilling and screaming.
The angry birds drop to the furrow, snatch at their food,
And lift again like torn papers blown in the wind.

Clive Sansom

Ploughing the Roughlands

It's not the four-wheeled drive crawler
spitting up dew and herbs,

not Dalapon followed by dressings
of dense phosphates,

nor ryegrass greening behind wire as behind glass,

not labourers wading in moonsuits
through mud gelded by paraquat—

but now, the sun-yellow, sky-blue
vehicles mount the pale chalk,

the sky bowls on the white hoops
and white breast of the roughland,

the farmer with Dutch eyes
guides forward the quick plough.

Now, flush after flush of Italian ryegrass
furs up the roughland

with its attentive, bright,
levelled-off growth—

pale monoculture
sweating off rivers of filth

fenced by the primary
colours of crawler and silo.

Helen Dunmore

The Ploughman

In these small fields
I have known the delight
Of being reborn each morning
And dying each night.

And I can tell
That birth and death
Are nothing so fierce
As the Preacher saith.

But when a life's but a day
The womb and tomb
Press lips in fondness
Like bride and groom.

And when a man's a ploughman
As I am now
An age is a furrow
And Time a plough,

And Infinity a field
That cannot stretch
Over the drain
Or through the ditch.

Patrick Kavanagh

Ploughman, Ploughman

Ploughman, ploughman, hold thy hand,
  Lead back to stall thy clanging team;
When poppies nod, leave thou the land
  To sleep awhile and dream.

When apple-scented chamomile
  Strains with her gold breast to the sun,
Gather thy apples, leave awhile
  The earth to slumber on.

By thriftless thrift men do not thrive;
  With autumn heat thy horses steam;
And O take heed how thou dost drive
  Thy plough across earth's dream.

Andrew Young

Ploughman and Whales

The ox went forward, a black block, eyes
                                    bulging,
The mouth a furnace.
Tammag went forward, cursing.
The plough wavered between them.
And gulls plagued Tammag, a whirl of
                              savage snow
On the field of the sun.
Twice the plough struck stone,
A clang like a bell
Between the burning hills and the cold sea.
Tammag clawed his shoulder. He cursed.
And the ox belched lessening flame.
Six furrows now and a bit. . .
Suddenly Tammag heard it, low thunder
Far in the firth,
And saw blue surging hills, the whales
On trek from ocean to ocean.
They plunged, they dipped, they wallowed,
They sieved a million small fish through
                                their teeth.
The sun stood at the hill, a black circle.
The shore erupted with men and boats,

A skirl of women,
Loud dogs, seaward asylums of gulls.
The ox stood in the seventh furrow
In a dream of grass and water.
'Tammag!' the boatman cried. 'Tammag!'
Tammag wiped his silver face on his sleeve.
 He yelled at the ox. The plough wavered.
                              They stumbled on.
They tore from the black sun
Loaf, honey-comb, fleece, ale-jar, fiddle.

George Mackay Brown

A Poet Visits
(for Yann)

Fields of foxy sorrel,
bedraggled nettle, ragwort,
yarrow juice on my hand.
'*A good place to sit,*'
                    you said.

Rain-mist drifts down hill,
hangs by the stream;
horses, muffled, shift and snort.
We reach out, floating, to touch the farthest tree.
'*My wife and I move house.*'

'*A poet should name all names of bird and flower.*'
You teach me "silena alba" for white campion.
—The summer trees turn bronze,
a scent of winter from the wood.
'*No poem for three months,*'
                    you said,
'*the vision comes and goes.*'

Frances Horovitz

The Poplar-Field

The poplars are fell'd, farewell to the shade
And the whispering sound of the cool colonnade,
The winds play no longer, and sing in the leaves,
Nor Ouse on his bosom their image receives.

Twelve years have elaps'd since I last took a view
Of my favourite field and the bank where they grew,
And now in the grass behold they are laid,
And the tree is my seat that once lent me a shade.

The blackbird has fled to another retreat
Where the hazels afford him a screen from the heat,
And the scene where his melody charm'd me before,
Resounds with his sweet-flowing ditty no more.

My fugitive years are all hasting away,
And I must ere long lie as lowly as they,
With a turf on my breast, and a stone at my head,
Ere another such grove shall arise in its stead.

'Tis a sight to engage me, if any thing can,
To muse on the perishing pleasures of man;
Though his life be a dream, his enjoyments, I see,
Have a being less durable even than he.

William Cowper

Question in a Field

Pasture, stone wall, and steeple,
What most perturbs the mind:
The heart-rending homely people,
Or the horrible beautiful kind?

Louise Bogan

Rhubarb Rhubarb

Return, return, O rhubarb fields,
That flourished in the days
When rhubarb fields gave proper yields
And Muck had proper praise:

When Fifty Tons of London dung
Each acre might expect;
And sweetly round the crowns it clung
To nourish and protect:

And wellfed Rhubarb, strong and fair,
And sure to make its price,
Hoisted great Clots of Muck in air—
Say what you like! I do not care!
I think it looked so nice!

Ruth Pitter

Riley

Down in the water-meadows Riley
Spread his wash on the bramble-thorn,
Sat, one foot in the moving water,
Bare as the day that he was born.

Candid was his curling whisker,
Brown his body as an old tree-limb,
Blue his eye as the jay above him
Watching him watch the minjies swim.

Four stout sticks for walls had Riley,
His roof was a rusty piece of tin,
As snug in the lew of a Cornish hedgerow
He watched the seasons out and in.

He paid no rates, he paid no taxes,
His lamp was the moon hung in the tree.
Though many an ache and pain had Riley
He envied neither you nor me.

Many a friend from bush or burrow
To Riley's hand would run or fly,
And soft he'd sing and sweet he'd whistle
Whatever the weather in the sky.

Till one winter's morning Riley
From the meadow vanished clean.
Gone was the rusty tin, the timber,
As if old Riley had never been.

What strange secret had old Riley?
Where did he come from? Where did he go?
Why was his heart as light as summer?
Never know now, said the jay. *Never know*.

Charles Causley

minjies: small minnows
lew: lee

St Luke's Summer

The low sun leans across the slanting field,
And every blade of grass is striped with shine
And casts its shadow on the blade behind,
And dandelion clocks are held
Like small balloons of light above the ground.

Beside the trellis of the bowling green
The poppy shakes its pepper-box of seed;
Groundsel feathers flutter down;
Roses exhausted by the thrust of summer
Lose grip and fall; the wire is twined with weed.

The soul, too, has its brown October days—
The fancy run to seed and dry as stone,
Rags and wisps of words blown through the mind;
And yet, while dead leaves clog the eyes,
Never-predicted poetry is sown.

Norman Nicholson

Scarecrow

Dressed in the farmer's ancient coat,
Worn, torn and tattered, night and day
He flutters in his field of wheat
To scare the strident rooks away.

His spine and hollow ribs are wood,
Wooden the legs he totters on,
And wood the jointed arm that holds
The barrel of a wooden gun.

When clods are brittle-bright with frost
Or in the sky a hot sun burns,
He haunts the field like a shabby ghost
And turns in the wind as the wind turns.

Clive Sansom

The Scarecrow

Stuck up? Maybe. But not proud
Of the job I do for the Lords of Creation.
They stuck me up, dressed me up in their clothes
To police their field, their garden, their orchard;
Never asking me whether I have a quarrel
With crow, starling or bullfinch. Take away
These cast-off togs I wear, and you'll find
I'm a soft old stick underneath, with no power.

It isn't for me to weigh up
The rights and wrongs of my function.
They sowed the crops, planted the trees I guard.
And they too have stripped this earth
Of the seed, the berries that once were natural food
For wild creatures. I'm sure of one thing only:
I do what I have to do. Stand where I'm put,
In the cold, in the heat, in the rain, with a straight face.
If I could smile I'd smile when some wily bird
Perches right on my hat, before getting down
To a good meal. But that couldn't happen.
If they thought it could, you'd never see me again.

Michael Hamburger

The Scarecrow

He strides across the grassy corn
That has not grown since it was born,
A piece of sacking on a pole,
A ghost, but nothing like a soul.

Why must this dead man haunt the spring
With arms anxiously beckoning?
Is spring not hard enough to bear
For one at autumn of his year?

Andrew Young

Scything

Gently we feel the edge of dawn creep forward
Between mist and pine.
Gently we swing the curved blade into the wet grass
Into the damp dew
Gently we edge knocked knees forward
Into the swathe.

Mowing ragwort and daisy
                smartweed and sorrell
                corncockle and chicory
Cutting, cutting, cutting close

Down to the roots, down to the moss
                timothy and foxtail
                cock's foot and fescue
                dog's tail and ryegrass.

Gently we swing the shoulders
        charlock and dodder
        sweet vernal and sowthistle
Bowing to the rhythm of the scythe
The meadow's pasture, the measured stride
Creeping forward into the shadow's singing.

SWISH SWISH SWISH SWISH

James Crowden

September

The first owls are working the dusk
on the upper field,
flitting back and forth along the hedge,
desultory and conversational
their low-pitched calls,
their sudden dips and turns.
This is a moment's grace, a stepping out
to gloaming, and the first breeze off the hills,
as I stand with my back to the wall
to feel the heat,
and listen, through the river of the trees,
for something of myself that waits to come,
as lyrical and poignant as the sound
of little owls and foxes on the hill
hunting for blood and warmth, in the yellow bracken.

John Burnside

Skylark

Suddenly above the fields you're pouring
Pure joy in a shower of bubbles,
Lacing the spring with the blue thread of summer.
You're the warmth of the sun in a song.

You're light spun to a fine filament;
Sun on a spider-thread—
That delicate.

You're the lift and balance the soul feels,
The terrible, tremulous, uncertain thrill of it—
You're all the music the heart needs,
Full of its sudden fall, silent fields.

Katrina Porteous

The Sky Lark

The rolls and harrows lies at rest beside
The battered road and spreading far and wide
Above the russet clods the corn is seen
Sprouting its spirey points of tender green
Where squats the hare to terrors wide awake
Like some brown clod the harrows failed to break
While neath the warm hedge boys stray far from home
To crop the early blossoms as they come
Where buttercups will make them eager run
Opening their golden caskets to the sun
To see who shall be first to pluck the prize
And from their hurry up the sky lark flies
And oer her half formed nest with happy wings
Winnows the air till in the clouds she sings
Then hangs a dust spot in the sunny skies
And drops and drops till in her nest she lies

Where boys unheeding past—neer dreaming then
That birds which flew so high would drop agen
To nests upon the ground where any thing
May come at to destroy had they the wing
Like such a bird themselves would be too proud
And build on nothing but a passing cloud
As free from danger as the heavens are free
From pain and toil—there would they build and be
And sail about the world to scenes unheard
Of and unseen—O where they but a bird
So think they while they listen to its song
And smile and fancy and so pass along
While its low nest moist with the dews of morn
Lies safely with the leveret in the corn

John Clare

The Soldier

If I should die, think only this of me:
   That there's some corner of a foreign field
That is for ever England. There shall be
   In that rich earth a richer dust concealed;
A dust whom England bore, shaped, made aware,
   Gave, once, her flowers to love, her ways to roam,
A body of England's, breathing English air,
   Washed by the rivers, blest by suns of home.

And think, this heart, all evil shed away,
   A pulse in the eternal mind, no less
     Gives somewhere back the thoughts by England given;
Her sights and sounds; dreams happy as her day;
   And laughter, learnt of friends; and gentleness,
     In hearts at peace, under an English heaven.

Rupert Brooke

Song

How sweet I roamed from field to field
  And tasted all the summer's pride,
Till I the prince of love beheld,
  Who in the sunny beams did glide.

He showed me lilies for my hair,
  And blushing roses for my brow;
He led me through his gardens fair,
  Where all his golden pleasures grow.

With sweet May dews my wings were wet,
  And Phoebus fired my vocal rage.
He caught me in his silken net,
  And shut me in his golden cage.

He loves to sit and hear me sing,
  Then laughing sports and plays with me—
Then stretches out my golden wing,
  And mocks my loss of liberty.

William Blake

Stacking the Straw

In those days the oatfields'
fenced-in vats of running platinum,
the yellower alloy of wheat and barley,
whose end, however gorgeous all that trammeled
rippling in the wind, came down
to toaster-fodder, cereal
as a commodity, were a rebuke
to permanence—to bronze or any metal
less utilitarian than the barbed braids

that marked off a farmer's property,
or the stoked dinosaur of a steam engine
that made its rounds from farm to farm,
after the grain was cut and bundled,
and powered the machine that did the threshing.

Strawstacks' beveled loaves, a shape
that's now extinct, in those days were
the nearest thing the region had
to monumental sculpture. While hayracks
and wagons came and went, delivering bundles,
carting the winnowed ore off to the granary,

a lone man with a pitchfork stood aloft
beside the hot mouth of the blower,
building about himself, forkful
by delicately maneuvered forkful,
a kind of mountain, the golden
stuff of mulch, bedding for animals.
I always thought of him with awe—
a craftsman whose evolving altitude
gave him the aura of a hero. He'd come down
from the summit of the season's effort
black with the baser residues of that
discarded gold. Saint Thomas of Aquino
also came down from the summit
of a lifetime's effort, and declared
that everything he'd ever done was straw.

Amy Clampitt

Struggling Wheat

(from the French of Jeanne Perdriel-Vassière)

Struggling wheat, weighed down with rain,
Which the sun scarce dries again,
Under a treacherous cloud unkind,
Between two passions of the wind:

Scanty wheat that cannot veil
The doomed nest and young of the quail
From the hawk that in the sky
Planes with ruin in his eye:

Child of the cold grudging clay,
Weeping when not parched away,
By the inconstant season harried
Even till you are cut and carried:

Still you strive with effort grim
To touch the overhanging limb
Of the tree that keeps the sun
For himself, and leaves you none.

Blackened wheat, and wheat of tears,
Earth besmirched and ruined ears,
Brave as an ill-fated man
Who does, though dying, what he can:

Take from this transient mind and eye
This look, this thought of sympathy;
Not leaden pity, but the love
Your gallant life is worthy of.

Ruth Pitter

Stubble Fires

Contours break the skin.
Acres of dust air
Drain from scraped fields:
White sheets bleaching to the hedge.

The rims harden
To bruised copper, violet,
Summer dead things,
A still shake of leaves.

East replies to West
In hems of ragged flame;
The darkening oils
Drift, merge, dissolve.

Ragnarok for the small gods.
Twilight wavers; cloaks
A shrivel of insects,
Morsels, burnt offerings.

And summer falls back, slips
Through policies of scorched earth.
Nostrils wince and prick
At charred roundels and striations.

An old ground-plan
Settles and clarifies
Land hurt and cleansed,
Picked to the black-bone.

Peter Scupham

The Sun used to Shine

The sun used to shine while we two walked
Slowly together, paused and started
Again, and sometimes mused, sometimes talked
As either pleased, and cheerfully parted

Each night. We never disagreed
Which gate to rest on. The to be
And the late past we gave small heed.
We turned from men or poetry

To rumours of the war remote
Only till both stood disinclined
For aught but the yellow flavorous coat
Of an apple wasps had undermined:

Or a sentry of dark betonies,
The stateliest of small flowers on earth,
At the forest verge: or crocuses
Pale purple as if they had their birth

In sunless Hades fields. The war
Came back to mind with the moonrise
Which soldiers in the east afar
Beheld then. Nevertheless, our eyes

Could as well imagine the Crusades
Or Caesar's battles. Everything
To faintness like those rumours fades—
Like the brook's water glittering

Under the moonlight—like those walks
Now—like us two that took them, and
The fallen apples, all the talks
And silences—like memory's sand

When the tide covers it late or soon,
And other men through other flowers
In those fields under the same moon
Go talking and have easy hours.

Edward Thomas

They are Ploughing

In the morning fields, where fiery red a spray
Of vine still burns in the hedge-row, and from bushes
The early mist like smoke is flowing away,

They are ploughing: one man urging on the slow
Cattle, slow-voiced, one sowing, one who pushes
The clods of earth back with his patient hoe.

And all they do the knowing sparrow watches,
Feasting in fancy, from its bramble hold,
And the robin sees, and out of woods and hedges
Sends its slight tinkling song that shines like gold.

E. J. Scovell

The Thing in the Gap-Stone Stile

I took the giant's walk on top of world,
peak-striding, each step a viaduct.

I dropped hankies, cut from a cloth of hills,
and beat gold under fields
for the sun to pick out a patch.

I never absolutely told
the curl-horned cows to line up their gaze.
But it happened, so I let it be.

And Annual Meadow Grass, quite of her own accord,
between the dry-stone spread out emerald.

(I was delighted by her initiative
and praised the dry-stone for being contrary.)

What I did do (I am a gap)
was lean these elbows on a wall
and sat on my hunkers pervading the boulders.

My pose became the pass across two kingdoms,
before behind antiphonal, my cavity the chord.

And I certainly intended
anyone to be almost
abstracted on a gap-stone between fields.

Alice Oswald

Thistle

Thistle, blue bunch of daggers
rattling upon the wind,
saw-tooth that separates
the lips of grasses.

Your wound in childhood was
a savage shock of joy
that set the bees on fire
and the loud larks singing.

Your head enchanted then
smouldering among the flowers
filled the whole sky with smoke
and sparks of seed.

Now from your stabbing bloom's
nostalgic point of pain
ghosts of those summers rise
rustling across my eyes.

Seeding a magic thorn
to prick the memory,
to start in my icy flesh
fevers of long lost fields.

Laurie Lee

Three Kinds of Pleasures

I

Sometimes, riding in a car, in Wisconsin
Or Illinois, you notice those dark telephone poles
One by one lift themselves out of the fence line
And slowly leap on the gray sky—
And past them, the snowy fields.

II

The darkness drifts down like snow on the picked cornfields
In Wisconsin: and on these black trees
Scattered, one by one,
Through the winter fields—
We see stiff weeds and brownish stubble,
And white snow left now only in the wheeltracks of the combine.

III

It is a pleasure, also, to be driving
Toward Chicago, near dark,
And see the lights in the barns.
The bare trees more dignified than ever,
Like a fierce man on his deathbed,
And the ditches along the road half full of a private snow.

Robert Bly

'Through all the meadows . . .'

Through all the meadows they are flowing,
To all the hilltops they are climbing:
Hedgerow and hedgerow and hedgerow.
Solemn and processional and shining,
In white garments they go.

To what intention are they plighted?
Where did they wash their festal apparel
So white, and so white, and so white?
What summoned out this maymonth nonpareil?
My despair, I say, and my delight.

From my astonished heart these votive
Hawthorns have come forth in procession,
Hedgerow after hedgerow after hedgerow!
In token of my release and my ransom
In thank-offering they go.

Sylvia Townsend-Warner

To a Fat Lady Seen from the Train
Triolet

O why do you walk through the fields in gloves,
  Missing so much and so much?
O fat white woman whom nobody loves,
Why do you walk through the fields in gloves,
When the grass is soft as the breast of doves
  And shivering-sweet to the touch?
O why do you walk through fields in gloves,
  Missing so much and so much?

Frances Cornford

To a Mouse
On turning her up in her nest with the plough,
November, 1785.

WEE, sleekit, cow'rin', tim'rous beastie,
O, what a panic's in thy breastie!
Thou need na start awa sae hasty,
            Wi' bickering brattle!
I wad be laith to rin an' chase thee,
            Wi' murd'ring pattle!

I'm truly sorry man's dominion
Has broken nature's social union,
An' justifies that ill opinion
            Which mak's thee startle
At me, thy poor earth-born companion,
            An' fellow-mortal!

I doubt na, whyles, but thou may thieve;
What then? poor beastie, thou maun live!
A daimen-icker in a thrave
            's a sma' request:

I'll get a blessin' wi' the lave,
And never miss't!

Thy wee bit housie, too, in ruin!
Its silly wa's the win's are strewin'!
An' naething, now, to big a new ane,
O' foggage green!
An' bleak December's winds ensuin',
Baith snell and keen!

Thou saw the fields lain bare an' waste,
An' weary winter comin' fast,
An' cozie here, beneath the blast,
Thou thought to dwell,
'Till, crash! the cruel coulter past
Out thro' thy cell.

That wee bit heap o' leaves an' stibble
Has cost thee mony a weary nibble!
Now thou's turn'd out, for a' thy trouble,
But house or hald,
To thole the winter's sleety dribble,
An' cranreuch cauld!

But, Mousie, thou art no thy lane,
In proving foresight may be vain:
The best laid schemes o' mice an' men,
Gang aft a-gley,
An' lea'e us nought but grief and pain
For promis'd joy.

Still thou art blest, compar'd wi' me!
The present only toucheth thee:
But, och! I backward cast my e'e,
On prospects drear!
An' forward, tho' I canna see,
I guess an' fear.

Robert Burns

Turnip-Heads

Here are the ploughed fields of Middle England;
and here are the scarecrows, flapping polythene arms
over what still, for the moment, looks like England:
bare trees, earth-colours, even a hedge or two.

The scarecrows' coats are fertilizer bags;
their heads (it's hard to see from the swift windows
of the Intercity) are probably 5-litre
containers for some chemical or other.

And what are the scarecrows guarding? Fields of rape?
Plenty of that in Middle England; also
pillage, and certain other medieval
institutions—some things haven't changed,

now that the men of straw are men of plastic.
They wave their rags in fitful semaphore,
in the March wind; our train blurs past them.
Whatever their message was, we seem to have missed it.

Fleur Adcock

'Up on the downs'

Up on the downs the red-eyed kestrels hover,
Eyeing the grass.
The field-mouse flits like a shadow into cover
As their shadows pass.

Men are burning the gorse on the down's shoulder;
A drift of smoke
Glitters with fire and hangs, and the skies smoulder,
And the lungs choke.

Once the tribe did thus on the downs, on these downs burning
Men in the frame,
Crying to the gods of the downs till their brains were turning
And the gods came.

And to-day on the downs, in the wind, the hawks, the grasses,
In blood and air,
Something passes me and cries as it passes,
On the chalk downland bare.

John Masefield

Up There

On Cotswold edge there is a field and that
Grows thick with corn and speedwell and the mat
Of thistles, of the tall kind; Rome lived there,
Some hurt centurion got his grant or tenure,
Built farm with fowls and pigsties and wood-piles,
Waited for service custom between whiles.
The farmer ploughs up coins in the wet-earth-time,
He sees them on the topple of crests gleam,
Or run down furrow; and halts and does let them lie
Like a small black island in brown immensity,
Till his wonder is ceased, and his great hand picks up the
penny.
Red pottery easy discovered, no searching needed. . . .
One wonders what farms were like, no searching needed,
As now the single kite hovering still
By the coppice there, level with the flat of the hill.

Ivor Gurney

The Viking Field

Not only thistles.

Gossamer: a shining network
woven before dawn.

Obstinate couch-grass
tall and blond
manning the ditches

and roses
tougher than they look,
craning their necks in hedgerows,
pale, shallow faces
following the sun's arc.

Scent of stone
and basting clumps of cow-dung.
Good warm glue.

A crinkle of silver foil
in the far corner.
Blind eye
flashing like a field of broken ice.

Day's breath bated.
Grass growing. The sound of it.
Sound of wool
growing on the lamb's back.

Systems of ants
stream out from their quarters
to inspect the field.

And even now
no dragons are forecast
for tonight,
but the candid sky
begins to congeal and sag.

Clover.
Wild garlic.
Ragged, unscrupulous crows.

Lance-leaves and heart-leaves,
tawny hairs, stinging.

Then all these spirit-wings:
this flickering assembly,
each silent woman flying
on her own,
double-headed axe.

Kevin Crossley-Holland

A Voice of Summer

In this one of all fields I know the best
All day and night, hoarse and melodious, sounded
A creeping corncrake, coloured like the ground,
Till the cats got him and gave the rough air rest.

Mechanical August, dowdy in the reeds,
He ground his quern and the round minutes sifted
Away in the powdery light. He would never lift
His beady periscope over the dusty hayseeds.

Cunning low-runner, tobogganing on his breast
He slid from sight once, from my feet. He only
Became the grass; then stone scraped harsh on stone,
Boxing the compass round his trivial nest.

—Summer now is diminished, is less by him.
Something that it could say cannot be spoken—
As though the language of a subtle folk
Had lost a word that had no synonym.

Norman MacCaig

Waiting for the Harvester

Here I stood in the crew-cut stubble,
Sharp stone in hand waiting for the harvester
To turn upon the final strip of wheat,
To see the hares dart wide-eyed into the gun's
Explosion or rise like crimson rags upon
The blades. Now, near the same spot, I can
Hardly recognise the self I was;
Now I am no longer armed—I move
Across the earth, mesmerised; myself
Trapped in the last small track of wilderness.
At every footfall, at every dog bark,
Every quiver of the vast machine, I shudder.
Sense in my flesh my own sharp stone;
The damp blades whirring above dry bone.

Peter Abbs

Walking on Sunday

In my wild yahooing days
When I was blowing about Alford,
Each fine-weather Sunday, walking was the treat
To watch for the express fish-train
Flashing through Well Fields into the beanfields beyond.
Dad said it went an hundred miles an hour,
And I, kite-clinging and credulous, believed him.
Sometimes we walked through Park Lane into ripe allotments
Full of shouting cockerels, pompous puff-balls of aggravation,
Then into the wide pastures beyond, yellow with buttercups,
All the way to the clear and sticklebacked beck.
The fields were fringed by secret thickets
Where the rabbits squealed as the weasels bit
And the half-ashamed foxes ran,
Shy and bold in turn, yet always sweet
To a boy's eyes. Sweet to a boy's mouth
Were the bright, black berries bleeding on the hand
And the bitter little hedge-plums, dusty green-fleshed sloes.
There were mushrooms, black and huge, to be gathered
Only to be metamorphosised into a creosote
Consumed by grown-ups, who never died from it.
Such was Sunday after-tea walking in my Dogdays.
Now the beck, remembered as a silver Zambesi,
Is pitifully small and fishless, broken-bridged and dead.
Uninteresting diesel fish trains crawl, and there's not
A single mushroom left, now that the shining horses have become
Sepia images in ancient photographs.
I, standing on my memories by the beck, threw no pebble.
I have changed a little, too . . .

N. S. Jackson

Watercolour of Grantchester Meadows

There, spring lambs jam the sheepfold. In air
Stilled, silvered as water in a glass
Nothing is big or far.
The small shrew chitters from its wilderness
Of grassheads and is heard.
Each thumb-size bird
Flits nimble-winged in thickets, and of good colour.

Cloudrack and owl-hollowed willows slanting over
The bland Granta double their white and green
World under the sheer water
And ride that flux at anchor, upside down.
The punter sinks his pole.
In Byron's pool
Cat-tails part where the tame cygnets steer.

It is a country on a nursery plate.
Spotted cows revolve their jaws and crop
Red clover or gnaw beetroot
Bellied on a nimbus of sun-glazed buttercup.
Hedging meadows of benign
Arcadian green
The blood-berried hawthorn hides its spines with white.

Droll, vegetarian, the water rat
Saws down a reed and swims from his limber grove,
While the students stroll or sit,
Hands laced, in a moony indolence of love—
Black-gowned, but unaware
How in such mild air
The owl shall stoop from his turret, the rat cry out.

Sylvia Plath

We Field-Women

How it rained
When we worked at Flintcomb-Ash,
And could not stand upon the hill
Trimming swedes for the slicing-mill.
The wet washed through us—plash, plash, plash:
How it rained!

How it snowed
When we crossed from Flintcomb-Ash
To the Great Barn for drawing reed,
Since we could nowise chop a swede.—
Flakes in each doorway and casement-sash:
How it snowed!

How it shone
When we went from Flintcomb-Ash
To start at dairywork once more
In the laughing meads, with cows three-score,
And pails, and songs, and love—too rash:
How it shone!

Thomas Hardy

'We have walked so many times, my boy'
To Den

We have walked so many times, my boy,
over these old fields given up
to thicket, have thought
and spoken of their possibilities,
theirs and ours, ours and theirs the same,
so many times, that now when I walk here
alone, the thought of you goes with me;
my mind reaches toward yours
across the distance and through time.

No mortal mind's complete within itself,
but minds must speak and answer,
as ours must, on the subject of this place,
our history here, summoned
as we are to the correction
of old wrong in this soil, thinned
and broken, and in our minds.

You have seen on these gullied slopes
the piles of stones mossy with age,
dragged out of furrows long ago
by men now names on stones,
who cleared and broke these fields,
saw them go to ruin, learned nothing
from the trees they saw return
to hold the ground again.

But here is a clearing we have made
at no cost to the world
and to our gain—a *re*-clearing
after forty years: the thicket
cut level with the ground,
grasses and clovers sown
into the last year's fallen leaves,
new pasture coming to the sun
as the woods plants, lovers of shade,

give way: change made
without violence to the ground.

At evening birdcall
flares at the woods' edge;
flight arcs into the opening
before nightfall.

Out of disordered history
a little coherence, a pattern
comes, like the steadying
of a rhythm on a drum, melody
coming to it from time
to time, waking over it,
as from a bird at dawn
or nightfall, the long outline
emerging through the momentary,
as the hill's hard shoulder
shows through trees
when the leaves fall.

The field finds its source
in the old forest, in the thicket
that returned to cover it,
in the dark wilderness of its soil,
in the dispensations of the sky,
in our time, in our minds—
the righting of what was done wrong.

Wrong was easy; gravity helped it.
Right is difficult and long.
In choosing what is difficult
we are free, the mind too
making its little flight
out from the shadow into the clear
in time between work and sleep.

There are two healings: nature's
and ours and nature's. Nature's
will come in spite of us, after us,
over the graves of its wasters, as it comes
to the forsaken fields. The healing
that is ours and nature's will come
if we are willing, if we are patient,
if we know the way, if we will do the work.
My father's father, whose namesake
you are, told my father this, he told me,
and I am telling you: we make
this healing, the land's and ours:
it is our possibility. We may keep
this place, and be kept by it.
There is a mind of such an artistry
that grass will follow it,
and heal and hold, feed beasts
who will feed us and feed the soil.

Though we invite, this healing comes
in answer to another voice than ours;
a strength not ours returns
out of death beginning in our work.

Though the spring is late and cold,
though uproar of greed
and malice shudders in the sky,
pond, stream, and treetop raise
their ancient songs;
the robin molds her mud nest
with her breast; the air
is bright with breath
of bloom, wise loveliness that asks
nothing of the season but to be.

Wendell Berry
'VI' *(1982)*

Woman in a Mustard Field

From love to light my element
was altered when I fled
out of your house to meet the space
that blows about my head.

The sun was rude and sensible,
the rivers ran for hours
and whoops I found a mustard field
exploding into flowers;

and I slowly came to sense again
the thousand forms that move
all summer through a living world
that grows without your love.

Alice Oswald

Acknowledgements

The idea of publishing an anthology of poetry about fields is not many publishers idea of a profitable proposition! Our deep thanks go to Satish Kumar and John Elford of Green Books for giving us the chance to show what richness is out there. If John Clare ". . . found the poems in the fields and only wrote them down . . ." then all we have done is to gather what we have found in the bookshelves.

We owe tremendous thanks to all the poets who have donated their poems for no fee, and for their encouragement, and to the publishers, agents and executors who have waived their fees.

We couldn't have hoped for a more appropriate person to write the foreword to this book. Adam Nicolson writes, with passion and conviction, a weekly page, 'The View from Perch Hill', in the *Sunday Telegraph Magazine*, often about his struggle with organic farming and the beauty and intricacy of his fields.

We couldn't have grazed the bookshelves for these poems without the existence of the Poetry Library at the South Bank Centre which holds a wonderful collection of twentieth century verse. Our intention has been to include the work of a large number of contemporary poets to reflect current thinking, but most libraries do not stock much late twentieth century poetry and most anthologies shy away from the complexities of copyright.

'Poetry Review', the journal of the Poetry Society, has been invaluable for introducing us to new poets and for its informative reviews of the work of some we are more familiar with. We should particularly like to thank John Greening for sending us 'My Meadow' by Hayden Carruth and Anne Stevenson for leading us to the work of Tom Rawling.

We are grateful too to our funders who enabled us to start the collection which has become this book. These include the Countryside Commission, Department of the Environment (as

it was then), London Boroughs Grants Committee, J. Paul
Getty Charitable Trust, the Elmgrant Trust and to Kathleen
Basford for her financial help and sustaining encouragement.
We should say that most of the work has been done out of
hours—a labour of love which has enriched us and our work.
We are also in debt to our Board of Directors for continually
challenging and supporting us.

Jane Kendall, Common Ground's Administrator and
Information Officer, has had the unenviable job of putting the
poems on the computer, of proof reading and making
corrections. She has done this diligently and cheerfully.
Without her work, this anthology wouldn't have been
possible. She has also made many suggestions for poems to be
included—for this very many thanks.

We apologise for any omissions or mistakes, for which we
take full responsibility.

Angela King and Sue Clifford
Common Ground

A-Z List of Poets and their Poems with Sources and Acknowledgements

Abbs, Peter, 1942-
Waiting for the Harvester
Personae and Other Selected Poems, Skoob Books, 1995.
© Peter Abbs 1995. Reproduced by permission of the author
and Skoob Books.

Adcock, Fleur, 1934-
Turnip Heads
Time Zones, Oxford University Press, 1991. © Fleur Adcock
1991. Reproduced by permission of the author and Oxford
University Press.

Anonymous
An Epitaph at Great Torrington, Devon
Voices, Book 2, edited by Geoffrey Summerfield, Penguin, 1968.

John Barleycorn
Voices, Book 1, edited by Geoffrey Summerfield, Penguin, 1968.

Barnes, William, 1801-1886
Home-Field
I Got Two Vields
William Barnes—The Dorset Poet, The Dovecote Press, 1984.
Reproduced by permission of The Dovecote Press.

Berry, Wendell, 1934-
Horses
A Part, North Point Press, 1980. © Wendell Berry 1980.
Reproduced by permission of the author and Farrar, Straus &
Giroux, Inc.

VI (1982) "We have walked so many times, my boy,"
Sabbaths, North Point Press, 1987. © Wendell Berry 1987.
Reproduced by permission of the author and Farrar, Straus &
Giroux, Inc.

Betjeman, John, 1906-1984
Harvest Hymn
Hertfordshire
The Licorice Fields of Pontefract
John Betjeman's Collected Poems, compiled by Lord
Birkenhead, John Murray, 1958/70. Reproduced by permission
of John Murray (Publishers) Ltd.

Bidgood, Ruth, 1922-
Meadow in Drought
The Print of Miracle, Gomer Press, Llandysul, Dyfed, 1978.
© Ruth Bidgood 1978. Reproduced by permission of the author.

Blake, William, 1757-1827
Song
The Poems of William Blake, edited by W. H. Stevenson,
Addison Wesley Longman, 1971. Reprinted by permission of
Addison Wesley Longman Ltd.

Bly, Robert, 1926-
Hunting Pheasants in a Corn Field
Three Kinds of Pleasures
Silence in the Snowy Fields, Wesleyan University Press,
Middleton, Ct., 1962. © Robert Bly 1962. Reprinted with the
permission of the author.

Bogan, Louise, 1897-1970
Question in a Field
The Blue Estuaries. © Ruth Limmer 1996. Reprinted with
permission of Farrar, Straus & Giroux, Inc.

Brackenbury, Alison, 1953-
Brockhampton
Linum
'*1829*', Carcanet Press, 1995. © Alison Brackenbury 1995.
Reproduced by permission of the author and Carcanet Press.

Brooke, Rupert, 1887-1915
The Soldier
The Poetical Works of Rupert Brooke, edited by Geoffrey
Keynes, Faber & Faber, 1946/1970.

Brown, George Mackay, 1921-1996
Black Furrow, Gray Furrow
Ploughman and Whales
Fishermen with Ploughs: A Poem Cycle, The Hogarth Press,
1971.
Reproduced by permission of John Murray (Publishers) Ltd.

Browning, Robert, 1812-1889
Home Thoughts from Abroad
Poetical Works 1833-1864, edited by Ian Jack, Oxford
University Press, 1970.

Bullett, Gerald, 1893-1958
A Field in June
An Exaltation of Skylarks, edited by Stewart Beer, SMH Books, 1995. © Mrs Rosemary Seymour.

Bunting, Basil, 1900-1985
O ubi campi!
The Complete Poems of Basil Bunting, Oxford University Press, 1994. Reproduced by permission of Oxford University Press.

Burns, Robert, 1759-1796
To a Mouse
The Poetical Works of Robert Burns, edited by John Fawside, Bliss, Sands & Foster, 1896.

Burnside, John, 1955-
On Merrow Down
An English Suite, The Hoop, Carcanet Press, 1988. © John Burnside 1988. Reproduced by permission of the author and Carcanet Press.

September
Swimming in the Flood, Jonathan Cape, 1995. © John Burnside 1995. Reproduced by permission of the author.

Carruth, Hayden, 1921-
My Meadow
Collected Shorter Poems 1946-1991, Copper Canyon Press. © Hayden Carruth 1992. Reprinted by permission of Copper Canyon Press, P.O. Box 271, Port Townsend, WA 98368.

Causley, Charles, 1917-
Riley
Collected Poems 1951-1997, Macmillan, London. Reprinted by permission of the author. © Charles Causley.

Clampitt, Amy, 1920-1994
Stacking the Straw
Collected Poems by Amy Clampitt. © 1997 by the Estate of Amy Clampitt. Reprinted by permission of Alfred A. Knopf Inc. and Faber & Faber.

Clare, John, 1793-1864
Grasshoppers
The Poems of John Clare, Volume 2, edited by J. W. Tibble, Dent, 1935. Reproduced by permission of J. M. Dent.

Hares at Play
The Mores
The Skylark
Selected Poems and Prose of John Clare, edited by Eric
Robinson & Geoffrey Summerfield, Oxford University Press,
1966. © Eric Robinson 1967. Reproduced with permission of
Curtis Brown Ltd, London, on behalf of Eric Robinson.

Clarke, Gillian, 1937-
Harvest at Mynachlog
Hay
Gillian Clarke: Collected Poems, Carcanet Press, 1997.
© Gillian Clarke 1997. Reproduced by permission of the author
and Carcanet Press.

Cornford, Frances, 1886-1960
Harvest
Poems by Frances Cornford, The Priory Press. © Frances
Cornford. Reproduced by permission of Enitharmon Press and
the Estate of Frances Cornford.

To a Fat Lady Seen from the Train
Selected Poems, edied by Jane Dowson, Enitharmon Press,
1996. © Frances Cornford. Reproduced by permission of
Enitharmon Press and the Estate of Frances Cornford.

Cowper, William, 1731-1800
The Poplar-Field
Cowper—The Poetical Works, edited by H. S. Milford, Oxford
University Press, 1905/67.

Crabbe, George, 1754-1832
'I grant indeed that fields and flowers have charms'
The Village, Book 1, Tales, 1812 and other Selected Poems,
edited by Howard Mills, Cambridge University Press, 1967.
Reproduced by permission of Cambridge University Press.

Crossley-Holland, Kevin, 1941-
Notes on a Field-Map
The Viking Field
The Language of Yes, Enitharmon Press, 1996. © Kevin
Crossley-Holland 1996. Reproduced by permission of the
author.

Crowden, James, 1954-
Harvest
Scything
Blood, Earth and Medicine, Parrett Press, 1991. © James
Crowden 1991. Reproduced by permission of the author and
The Parrett Press.

Crucefix, Martyn, 1956-
The Gleaners
Beneath Tremendous Rain, Enitharmon Press, 1990. © Martyn
Crucefix 1990. Reproduced by permission of the author.

Davie, Donald, 1922-1995
The Hill Field
Selected Poems, Carcanet Press, 1997. Reproduced by
permission of Carcanet Press.

Davies, W. H., 1870-1940
Advice
Beggar's Luck
Cowslips and Larks
A Happy Life
The Complete Poems of W. H. Davies, Jonathan Cape, 1916/63.
Reproduced by permission of the Executors of the W. H. Davies
Estate and Jonathan Cape.

Dooley, Maura
Over the Fields
Explaining Magnetism, Bloodaxe Books, 1986/1991. © Maura
Dooley 1986/1991. Reproduced by permission of the author
and Bloodaxe Books.

Duffy, Maureen, 1933-
Burning Off
Collected Poems 1949-84, Hamish Hamilton, 1985. © Maureen
Duffy 1985. Reproduced by permission of the author.

Dunmore, Helen, 1952-
New Crops
Ploughing the Roughlands
Short Days Long Nights: New and Selected Poems, Bloodaxe
Books, 1991. © Helen Dunmore 1991. Reproduced by
permission of the author and Bloodaxe Books.

Eliot, T. S., 1888-1965
'In that open field'
from 'East Coker', *Four Quartets, Collected Poems 1909-1962,*
Faber & Faber. Reproduced by permission of the Eliot Estate,
Faber & Faber and Harcourt, Brace & Company.

Fainlight, Ruth, 1931-
The Field
Selected Poems, Sinclair-Stevenson, 1995. © Ruth Fainlight
1995. Reproduced by permission of the author.

Frost, Robert, 1874-1963
Mowing
The Poetry of Robert Frost, edited by Edward Connery Lathem,
© 1962 by Robert Frost. © 1934, 1969 by Henry Holt &
Company, Inc. Reprinted by permission of Henry Holt and
Company, Inc.

Garfitt, Roger, 1944-
Hares Boxing
Given Ground, Carcanet Press, 1989. © Roger Garfitt 1989.
Reproduced by permission of Roger Garfitt and Carcanet Press
Ltd.

Gillilan, Pamela
Harvest
All Steel Traveller, New & Selected Poems, Bloodaxe Books,
1986/94. © Pamela Gillilan 1986, 1994. Reproduced by
permission of the author and Bloodaxe Books.

Graves, Robert, 1895-1985
Lost Acres
Complete Poems, Carcanet Press 1995. Reproduced by
permission of Carcanet Press.

Greening, John, 1954-
Barrow
Fotheringhay and other Poems, Rockingham Press, 1995. ©
John Greening 1995. Reproduced by permission of the author.

Grigson, Geoffrey, 1905-1985
No Sprinkling of Bright Weeds
Collected Poems 1963-80, Alison & Busby, 1982. Reproduced
by permission of David Higham Associates Ltd.

Gurney, Ivor, 1890-1937
Brown Earth Look
Friendly are Meadows
In December
Up There
Collected Poems of Ivor Gurney, chosen & edited by
P. J. Kavanagh, Oxford University Press, 1984. Reproduced by
permission of Oxford University Press.

Hamburger, Michael, 1924-
Bread and Butter Letter
The Scarecrow
Michael Hamburger: Collected Poems 1941-94, published by
Anvil Press Poetry, 1995. © Michael Hamburger 1995.
Reproduced by permission of the author and Anvil Press Poetry.

Hardy, Thomas, 1840-1928
We Field-Women
The Complete Poems of Thomas Hardy, edited by James Gibson,
Papermac, 1976. Reproduced by permission of Macmillan.

Hart, David. 1940-
Naming the Fields
Winner, Field Days Poetry Competition, Blue Nose Poets /
Common Ground, 1997/8. © David Hart 1997. Reproduced by
permission of the author.

Heaney, Seamus, 1939-
Glanmore Sonnets 1
New Selected Poems, 1966-1987, Faber & Faber, 1990. ©
Seamus Heaney 1990. Reproduced by permission of the author,
Farrar, Straus & Giroux, Inc. and Faber & Faber.

Herrick, Robert, 1591-1674
To Meddowes
The Poetical Works of Robert Herrick, edited by F. W.
Moorman, Oxford University Press, 1915.

Hooker, Jeremy, 1941-
Flints
The Invisible Globe
Soliloquies of a Chalk Giant, Enitharmon Press, 1974. © Jeremy
Hooker 1974. Reproduced by permission of Enitharmon Press.

Gander Down
A Master of the Leaping Figures, Enitharmon Press, 1987.
© Jeremy Hooker 1987. Reproduced by permission of
Enitharmon Press.

Hopkins, Gerard Manley, 1844-1889
Pied Beauty
The Poems of Gerard Manley Hopkins, edited by W. H.
Gardner & N. H. Mackenzie, Oxford University Press 1967,
1970.

Horovitz, Frances, 1938-1983
A Poet Visits
Collected Poems, Bloodaxe Books, 1985. Reproduced by
permission of Bloodaxe Books.

Jackson, Norman
Fieldwalking
Fieldwalking, Bran's Head Books, 1983. © Norman Jackson
1983. Reproduced by permission of the author.

Jackson, N. S., 1928-1993
Walking on Sunday
Poems by N.S. Jackson, edited by Robert Christian,
Lincolnshire & South Humberside Arts, 1974. Reproduced by
permission of
S. M. Jackson.

Jarrell, Randall, 1914-1965
Field and Forest
The Complete Poems, Faber & Faber, 1971. © Mrs Randall
Jarrell 1969. Reproduced by permission of Farrar, Straus &
Giroux, Inc. and Faber & Faber.

Jennings, Elizabeth, 1926-
English Wild Flowers
A Dream of Spring, Celandine Press, 1980. © Elizabeth
Jennings 1980. Reproduced by permission of David Higham
Associates Ltd.

Kavanagh, P. J., 1931-
Farmworker
Presences. New and Selected Poems, Chatto & Windus, 1987.
© P. J. Kavanagh 1987. Reproduced by permission of the author
and Carcanet Press Ltd.

Kavanagh, Patrick, 1904-1967
The Ploughman
Selected Poems, Penguin, 1996. Reproduced by kind permission
of the Trustees of the Estate of Patrick Kavanagh, c/o Peter
Fallon, Literary Agent, Loughcrew, Oldcastle, Co. Meath,
Ireland.

Keats, John, 1795-1821
On the Grasshopper and Cricket, December 30, 1816
The Poetical Works of John Keats, edited by H. Buxton
Forman, Reeves & Turner, 1902.

Kipling, Rudyard, 1865-1936
The Land
The Complete Verse, Kyle Cathie, 1990. © Rudyard Kipling
1990.
Reproduced by permission of A. P. Watt Ltd on behalf of The
National Trust.

Langland, William, c.1332-1400
'In a summer season when the sun was mild'
The Vision of Piers Plowman, translated by E. Talbot
Donaldson in *The School Bag*, edited by Seamus Heaney & Ted
Hughes, Faber & Faber, 1997.

Lee, Laurie, 1914-1997
Thistle
Selected Poems, Penguin Books, 1983. Permission granted by
Peters Fraser & Dunlop Ltd.

Levertov, Denise, 1923-1997
By Rail through the Earthly Paradise, Perhaps Bedfordshire
The Cabbage Field
In Summer
Selected Poems, Bloodaxe Books, 1986. Reprinted by
permission of Laurence Pollinger Ltd and New Directions
Publishing Corporation.

MacBeth, George, 1932-1992
The Field, Tomorrow
Collected Poems, 1958-82, Hutchinson, 1989. Reproduced by
permission of Huchinson and Shiel Land Associates.

MacCaig, Norman, 1910-1996
Fetching Cows
A Voice of Summer
Collected Poems, Chatto & Windus, 1985. Reproduced by
permission of The Hogarth Press.

McCrae, John, 1872-1918
In Flanders Fields
More Poetry Please!, J. M. Dent, 1991.

Martinson, Harry Edmund, 1904-
The Earthworm (translated from the Swedish by Robert Bly)
from 'Friends, You Drank Some Darkness' in *The Rattle Bag*,
edited by Ted Hughes & Seamus Heaney, Faber & Faber, 1982.
© Robert Bly 1975. Reprinted by permission of Robert Bly.

Masefield, John, 1878-1967
Up on the Downs
Poems by John Masefield, Heinemann, 1923/61. Reproduced by
permission of The Society of Authors as the Literary
Representative of the Estate of John Masefield.

Mew, Charlotte, 1869-1928
In the Fields
The Rambling Sailor (1929), Collected Poems & Prose, edited
with an introduction by Val Warner, Carcanet Press, 1981.
Reproduced by permission of Carcanet Press.

Nicholson, Norman, 1914-1987
Millom Cricket Field
The New Cemetery
St Luke's Summer
Collected Poems, edited by Neil Curry, Faber & Faber, 1994.
Reproduced by permission of David Higham Associates.

Oswald, Alice, 1966-
The Thing in the Gap-Stone Stile
Woman in a Mustard Field
The Thing in the Gap-Stone Stile, Oxford University Press,
1996. © Alice Oswald 1996. Reproduced by permission of the
author and Oxford University Press.

Pitter, Ruth, 1897-1992
Rhubarb Rhubarb
Struggling Wheat (from the French of Jeanne Perdriel-Vassiere)
Collected Poems, introduced by Elizabeth Jennings, Enitharmon
Press, 1996. Reproduced by permission of the Estate of Ruth
Pitter CBE and Enitharmon Press.

Plath, Sylvia, 1932-1963
Watercolour of Grantchester Meadows
The Colossus and Other Poems, Faber & Faber, 1960/72.
© 1960 by Sylvia Plath. Reproduced by permission of Alfred A.
Knopf Inc. and Faber & Faber.

Porteous, Katrina, 1960-
Skylark
The Lost Music, Bloodaxe Books 1996. © Katrina Porteous
1996. Reproduced by permission of the author.

Raine, Kathleen, 1908-
Childhood Memory
Selected Poems, Golgonooza Press, 1988
© Kathleen Raine 1988. Reproduced by permission of the
author and Golgonooza Press.

Rawling, Tom, 1916-1996
The Old Showfield
The Old Showfield, Taxus, 1984. Included by permission of his
daughters: Mrs Sue Slater and Rev. Jane Rawling.

Read, Herbert, 1893-1968
April
Pasturelands
Selected Poetry, Sinclair-Stevenson, 1966. Reproduced by
permission of David Higham Associates.

Reed, Jeremy, 1951-
Neutral
Selected Poems, Penguin, 1984. © Jeremy Reed 1984.
Reproduced by permission of the author.

Rodgers, W R, 1909-1969
Field Day
Poems, The Gallery Press, 1993. Reproduced by permission of
The Gallery Press.

Rossetti, Christina, 1830-1894
'Consider the Lilies of the Field'
The Complete Poems of Christina Rossetti, edited by R. W.
Crump, Louisiana State University Press, 1979.

Rowse, A. L., 1903-1997
Cornish Acre
A Life, Collected Poems, Blackwood, 1981. Reproduced by
permission of John Johnson (Authors' Agent) Ltd.

Sansom, Clive, 1910-1981
Field Names
Dorset Village, Methuen, 1962. Reproduced by permission of
David Higham Associates.

Ploughing
Scarecrow
An English Year, Chatto & Windus, 1975. Reproduced by
permission of David Higham Associates.

Scovell, E. J., 1907-
The Clover Fields
A Field
They are Ploughing
Collected Poems, Carcanet Press, 1988. © E. J. Scovell 1988.
Reproduced by permission of Carcanet Press.

Scupham, Peter, 1933-
Stubble Fires
Summer Places, Oxford University Press, 1980.
© Peter Scupham 1980. Reproduced by permission of Oxford
University Press.

Thomas, Edward, 1878-1917
Haymaking
The Sun used to Shine
Collected Poems by Edward Thomas, edited by R. George
Thomas, Oxford University Press. Reproduced by permission of
Myfanwy Thomas and Oxford University Press.

Thomas, R. S., 1913-
The Bright Field
Later Poems 1972-82, Macmillan, 1972-83. © R. S. Thomas
1972-83. Reproduced by permission of the author.

Cynddlyan on a Tractor
Collected Poems 1945-1990, J. M. Dent, 1993. © R. S. Thomas
1993. Reproduced by permission of the author.

Thwaite, Anthony, 1930-
The Barrow
Poems 1953-1988, Hutchinson, 1989. © Anthony Thwaite
1989. Reproduced by permission of the author.

Townsend-Warner, Sylvia, 1893-1978
'Through all the Meadows . . .'
Collected Poems, edited by Claire Harman, Carcanet New
Press, 1982. Reproduced by permission of Carcanet Press.

Virgil, 70BC-19BC
'In early spring, when the ice on the snowy mountains'
The Georgics, Book 1, translated by L. P. Wilkinson, Penguin
Books, 1982. © L. P. Wilkinson 1982. Reproduced by
permission of Penguin Books Ltd.

Watkins, Vernon, 1906-1967
The Mare
Collected Poems, Golgonooza Press, 1986. Reproduced by
permission of G. M. Watkins.

Whitman, Walt, 1819-1892
As I Watch'd the Ploughman Ploughing
The Complete Poems, edited by Francis Murphy, Penguin
1975/82.

Wiseman, Christopher, 1936-
The Field
first appeared in *The Upper Hand*, Enitharmon Press, 1981 and
in *Postcards Home: Poems New and Selected*, Sono Nis Press
(Canada), 1988. © Christopher Wiseman 1981, 1988. Published
with permission of the author.

Young, Andrew, 1885-1971
In the Fallow Field
On the Hill
Ploughman, Ploughman
The Scarecrow
Complete Poems, Secker & Warburg, 1974. Reproduced by
permission of Carcanet Press.

Common Ground have used their best endeavours to trace all the
holders of copyright in the poems that are not in the public domain,
but have been unable to locate a small number of the poets, their
heirs or estates. Common Ground will be glad to hear from any such
copyright-holders.

About Common Ground

Common Ground offers ideas, information and inspiration to help people to learn about, enjoy and take more responsibility for their own locality.

In the spectrum of environmental organisations Common Ground uniquely pioneers imaginative work on nature, culture and place. We link people, landscape, wild life, buildings, history and customs as well as bridging philosophy and practice, environment and the arts.

We explore new ways of looking at the world to excite people into remembering the richness of everyday landscapes, common wild life and ordinary places, to savour the symbolisms with which we have endowed nature, to revalue our emotional engagement with places and all that they mean to us, and to go on to become involved in their care.

In raising awareness and action through model projects, exhibitions, publications and events we are attempting to create a popular culture of wanting to care: we believe that the only way in which we shall achieve a sustainable relationship with nature is by everyone taking part in the effort. 'Holding Your Ground: an action guide to local conservation', 1985, established our role in informing local environmental action and cultural expression.

In reasserting the importance of liberating our subjective response to the world about us, we often work with people for whom this is everyday currency—poets, sculptors, composers, painters, writers, performers—people from all branches of the arts.

Common Ground is a charity (Charity No. 326335), formed in 1983. We seek no members and create no structures. Through collaborations we build links between organisations and disciplines, local people and professionals. We act as a catalyst and mentor; by broadcasting ideas and demonstrating by example we try to extend the constituencies for conservation and create foundations for real democracy.

Our projects include the Campaign for Local Distinctiveness; Field Days; Trees, Woods & the Green Man; Save our Orchards; Apple Day (October 21st); Tree Dressing Day (1st weekend in December); Parish Maps; local *Flora Britannica*; New Milestones; Rhynes, Rivers & Running Brooks; and Confluence.

Common Ground's Manifesto for Fields

Fields have meanings and memories for millions of us. In their manifold forms, fields express our cultural crafting of the land. They are our unwritten history, carved clearings in the wild wood, the accumulation of practical experimentation, invention and subtlety, extending over generations. Yet under our gaze this rich combining of culture and nature has been smoothed and sprayed out of existence in half a lifetime.

There is something fundamentally wrong with the way we treat the land now. We have lost the wisdom of the fields.

Deep ploughing has reduced ridge and furrow, buried villages and countless barrows. Only 13% of our stonewalls are still stockproof; 209,000 miles of hedge were removed between 1947 and 1990. Agricultural intensification and development have caused the demise of 97% of our hay meadows, 80% of our chalk and limestone downlands, and 65% of our Culm grasslands during the last 25 years.

Over the same period, and for allied reasons, farmland bird populations have declined drastically—the native grey partridge by 82%, spotted flycatcher by 73%, lapwing by 62% and skylark by 58%.

People have disappeared from the land too. Between 1983 and 1994 the agricultural labour force fell from 616,000 to 538,000. Now only 2.1% of the workforce in Britain is involved in agriculture. Farms have become larger; so have farm machines, The result has been increasing isolation and pressure for those left to work the land. More farmers kill themselves in Britain than in any other occupation. The Samaritans say that suicide is now the second most common cause of death in farmers under 45 years.

As agriculture has become more mechanised and intensive, it has become more remote and more excluding; people even feel unable to engage in debate about it.

HOLISTIC farming—working with nature, culture and locality, rotating crops, mixing livestock with arable production and reducing our dependence on artificial pesticides, herbicides and fertilisers—could solve many problems. If farmers produced food for local consumption they would be in direct contact with the surrounding community and would be more likely to be valued and understood. Local distinctiveness would be reinforced, culture and nature once more particularising place.

We need to re-think what fields are for, if we want them to continue to fulfil a wider role than just crop and livestock production. Fields are not factories—they are our unique and variegated expression of a long relationship with the land.

What do we want fields to be, look like and sustain? Grants to farmers and landholders have enabled and encouraged most of the detrimental changes to the land. As taxpayers, we are footing the bill for massive subsidies—£3.3 billion in 1996.

These grants benefit a few, not society as a whole. They have led to the destruction of our common wealth—our wildlife inheritance, evidence of the way we have worked the land over millennia, the pollution of watercourses and the reduction of the intrinsic potential of the soil.

Fields should be full of life, we should be working with this natural exuberance and diversity rather than trying to suppress it.

Changes to the way we treat the land will only come from popular pressure. If you share this belief with us, send for *A Manifesto for Fields*, £3.50 + p&p, which is a provocation to thought and action and, if your manifesto resembles ours, then please write to the Minister for Agriculture, Fisheries and Food, Whitehall Place, London, SW1A 2HH, to your MP and MEP. Demand that support for agriculture should only be available if it produces wholesome food, reflects and reinforces the cultural importance of fields, improves conditions for farmworkers and benefits society, the welfare of livestock, nature and the land.

Though nothing can bring back the hour
Of splendour in the grass, of glory in the flower;
                We will grieve not, rather find
                Strength in what remains behind

                              William Wordsworth

Publications by Common Ground

A MANIFESTO FOR FIELDS makes 41 arguments for fairer fields. A5, 24 pages with illustrations by leading artists. 1997. £3.50. + 50p p&p.

FIELD DAYS: Ideas for Investigations and Celebrations, is packed with a wide range of suggestions, ideas and examples, to encourage Field Day activities, from surveys to picnics, promoting a greater awareness of the importance of fields and active local participation in their future. A5, 24 pages with illustrations by leading artists. 1997. £3.50 + 50p p&p.

LOCAL DISTINCTIVENESS: Place, Particularity and Identity, essays for a conference, including papers by Richard Mabey, Gillian Darley, Neal Ascherson, Patrick Wright, Michael Dower and Roger Deakin. 1993. £5.95. + £1.50 p&p.

CELEBRATING LOCAL DISTINCTIVENESS, Common Ground for Rural Action. Gives examples of how local people are reinforcing local identity. Provides anyone with an interest in environmental action and arts in rural areas with a fascinating gathering of examples that are both persuasive and practical. 1994. £3.00 + 50p p&p

FROM PLACE TO PLACE: Maps and Parish Maps. Writings about maps and places. Sets the scene for an idea which challenges communities to explore, express and care for the things they value in their everyday places. Writers including Barbara Bender, Robin Grove-White, Simon Lewty, Richard Mabey and Adam Nicolson are joined by people describing their experiences of Parish Mapping. 1996. £10.00 + £1.50 p&p.

THE APPLE SOURCE BOOK, Particular Recipes for Diverse Apples. Leading cooks, chefs, gardeners and writers offer old and new recipes. They widen our horizons to the wealth of apples which we could be using to enrich both our culinary and cultural landscapes. 1991. £4.95 + £1.50 p&p.

APPLE GAMES AND CUSTOMS, foreword by Sophie Grigson. This book will help you to sip from a huge wassail bowl of games, customs, sayings and stories which remind us of the importance and meaning which the apple has in our culture, We hope it will inspire you to carry on the traditions of your own locality, and help build Apple Day on October 21st into a new calendar custom. B/w illustrations. 1994. £5.95. + £1.50 p&p.

Overseas orders: please pay in sterling (international money order or traveller's cheques), allowing substantial postage costs. For information on other publications please send s.a.e. to:

COMMON GROUND, PO BOX 25309, LONDON NW5 1ZA, UK